Radiance of the Heart

KINDNESS, COMPASSION, BODHICITTA

Ringu Tulku Rinpoche

Compiled & edited by Mary Heneghan

BODHICHARYA PUBLICATIONS

Bodhicharya Publications is a Community Interest Company registered in the UK.

38 Moreland Avenue, Hereford, HR1 1BN, UK

www.bodhicharya.org   Email: publications@bodhicharya.org

© Bodhicharya Publications 2018

Ringu Tulku asserts the moral right to be identified as the author of this work.

Please do not reproduce any part of this book without permission from the publisher.

ISBN 978-0-9957343-1-9

First Edition: January 2018, Tibetan Year of the Female Fire Bird

Compiled and edited by Mary Heneghan

Teaching sources:

The Story of the Cobbler and the Angel, taken from: *Four Limitlessnesses*. Given at Dzogchen Beara, Ireland. April 2008.

Bringing Kindness and Compassion into our Daily Lives, and some Questions and Answers, taken from: *Simple Magic: Bringing Kindness and Compassion into Daily Life, with a look at Tonglen*. Given at Friends Meeting House, Oxford, UK. May 2017.

Further Questions and Answers, taken from: *'Relative and Ultimate Bodhicitta, from theory to practice.'* Given at Palpung Changchub Dargyeling, Wales, UK. June 2016. And *Retreat Teachings* given at Bodhicharya Meditation Centre with Donal Creedon, Sikkim, India. January 2017.

Kindness and Compassion from an Ultimate Perspective, taken from: *'Relative and Ultimate Bodhicitta, from theory to practice.'* Given at Palpung Changchub Dargyeling, Wales, UK. June 2016.

All transcribed and edited by Mary Heneghan.

Bodhicharya Publications team for this book: Mary Heneghan; Anne Howard; Rachel Moffitt; Paul O'Connor; Maeve O'Sullivan; Mariette van Lieshout.

Typesetting & Design by Paul O'Connor at www.judodesign.com

Cover image: Sunrise, taken over Japan, by Masyok.

Printed on recycled paper by Imprint Digital, Devon, UK.

The Heart Wisdom Series
By Ringu Tulku Rinpoche

The Ngöndro
Foundation Practices of Mahamudra

From Milk to Yoghurt
A Recipe for Living and Dying

Like Dreams and Clouds
Emptiness and Interdependence, Mahamudra and Dzogchen

Dealing with Emotions
Scattering the Clouds

Journey from Head to Heart
Along a Buddhist Path

Riding Stormy Waves
Victory over the Maras

Being Pure
The practice of Vajrasattva

Radiance of the Heart
Kindness, Compassion, Bodhicitta

*'In this world, hate never yet dispelled hate.
Only love dispels hate.
This is the law, ancient and inexhaustible.'* [1]

Contents

Editor's Preface	xiii
The Story of the Cobbler and the Angel	1
Bringing Kindness and Compassion into our Daily Lives	7
Being aware	8
Clarifying our view	10
Wishing well, warm heartedness	11
Choosing your action wisely	12
You have to be strong to be kind	13
A natural quality	14
The practice of *tonglen*	15
Dare to breathe in what you fear	16
Dare to give away what you value	17
Being free to be kind	18
The solution to all the problems in the world	18
We have to do it	19
Negative emotions, letting them go	20
The one true antidote	22
Questions & Answers	25
Kindness, compassion and Bodhicitta	26
Meditating on kindness and facing fear	28
Connecting with tonglen practice	30
Helping ourselves, and helping others, through practice	32
'Justified anger'	34

Compassion for people it is hard to feel compassion for	35
Wrathful compassion	37
Taking a vow to become a Bodhisattva	37
Expecting gratitude	38
'Mixed-up' motivation	39
Healing yourself before helping others?	40
The story of the woman who lost her son	42
Renunciation, attachment and love	44
Choices	45
Helping the elderly	47
A purposeful life	48
'Compassion fatigue' and empathy	49
Relative and Ultimate Bodhicitta	53

Kindness and Compassion From an Ultimate Perspective   59

Seeds of boundless love and compassion	60
Understanding Ultimate Bodhicitta	64
Approaching Ultimate Bodhicitta	69
Moments	72
Meditating on Ultimate Bodhicitta	76
Paths to realisation	79

Glossary and Notes	87
Acknowledgements	95
About the Author	97
Other books by Ringu Tulku	98

Editor's Preface

There is nothing so transformative in a day, as a little kindness. And over the length of our whole lives, too, what really touches us? What really moves and influences us more than anything? Possibly the moments we are lucky enough to experience true kindness and compassion; genuine care and interest; love.

This topic is truly central for all of us, whether we know it or not. A kind act or a benevolent wish, such delicately simple movements of the heart: so precious, so uncomplicated in a way - how is it that we lose touch with this natural feeling so easily? Ringu Tulku is often asked to teach on these topics for just this reason. We all need to hear such teaching over and over again, at each point in our lives.

This is why we have endeavoured to put together this small text, and bring together here as much of Rinpoche's teaching on this matter as we could. It is hoped these teachings will help us reconnect again and again to that which is our hearts' natural texture and quality, and let the kindness inherent in us all shine, and radiate out.

We can approach this subject in different ways. As with many things in life, and in the Dharma Buddha taught, we can look at it in a relative, provisional, practical way. Or we can look into it in a more penetrative or 'ultimate' way. 'Relative' explanations may be to some extent provisional, but they give us a way to work with things in an everyday, practical sense. We can understand and apply these teachings directly, where we are currently at and how life generally seems to be for us.

An 'ultimate' approach investigates deeper, more philosophical issues, to do with how we see things, how things ultimately exist. It works with the ways in which our understanding is limited and yet can be deepened over time, bringing our everyday view and actions into alignment with ever deeper and clearer truths.

Maybe it is helpful to say here that, when we talk about relative and ultimate approaches, it is not that there is a relative thing and that there is an ultimate thing, as if they were separate or different. *There just is what there is.* The relative and the ultimate are ways of talking about or understanding or relating with 'what is.' And both these approaches are helpful. Neither negates the other and neither can be fully developed without the other. They flow into one another, inform each other and intimately co-exist, seamlessly.

This is inherent in how the Buddha taught the Dharma: in more than one 'turning of the wheel of Dharma.' Firstly, the foundational truths were given, ones we can work with in a practical and immediate way. These were developed later, in successive turnings of the wheel - successive rounds of teaching - to reveal an increasingly ultimate perspective. Developing this ultimate view allows one to revisit the foundational teachings and find within them greater and greater meaning; perhaps finding that everything was within them already, only that now we can see it.

It is the same with the core teachings on kindness and compassion. His Holiness the Dalai Lama is often heard to say, 'My religion is compassion.' Compassion and kindness are the very bedrock of Buddhism, and possibly the true expression of every religion. The essence of human kindness ties us all together, whether expressed within a religion or through contributing to the happiness and wholesome development of society in general. Wherever kindness and compassion are the guiding motivation, there is a certain quality that starts to emerge, and this quality sustains and suffuses life with joy and peace and a sense of abundance. What is the texture of this quality? It is called Bodhicitta in the Buddhadharma.

Bodhi means 'awake' and *citta* refers to the heart-mind, the essence of our being. When our essential nature is fully realised or awakened, compassion and kindness are found to be its natural expression. They are not things that have to be created or fabricated. So, the more we can encourage ourselves to embody kindness and compassion, the closer we get to our true nature. These qualities are naturally present, needing only to be awakened, nurtured and allowed to fully blossom. This in turn brings great wisdom, and great wisdom brings further, boundless, kindness and compassion.

So, both the practical and the deeper philosophical approaches are equally important. If we neglect the day-to-day expression of kindness and compassion, we overlook our whole life, where we actually live and where we can make a difference. Ringu Tulku explains these teachings are most important because they are foundational - they are teachings we can easily understand and so we can bring them into our lives right now. Without this practical understanding, any further philosophical understanding is only that: philosophical; it can never become grounded in experience without these core teachings becoming part of ourselves.

If we neglect trying to understand the deeper nature of things, we create a restriction in ourselves, a limitation or 'ceiling,' which will always curtail and confuse the depth and expression of our kindness. If we open to exploring this deeper level of understanding, it can eventually lead us to a place where compassion spontaneously arises of its own accord, in a purely uncontrived way. We start to experience how everything exists in a vastly interconnected and inter-related way; and so we start to open into a freer flow between everything, which is none other than a space of kindness and love.

So, we are very happy to present some of Ringu Tulku's precious and extensive teachings on kindness and compassion, here in this Heart Wisdom book. In keeping with the outline above, the book is presented in distinct parts: approaching the subject from the relative, and later the ultimate, points of view. We start with Rinpoche's retelling of Tolstoy's story *Human Beings Live by the Love of Others*. This is how Rinpoche started his teachings at Dzogchen Beara on the Four Limitless Qualities [of Loving-Kindness, Compassion, Joy and Equanimity] and it sets the scene for our own learning here.

Then we go on to *Bringing Kindness and Compassion into our Daily Lives*, which contains day-to-day essential teaching, which we can start to put into practice this very day. The *Question and Answer* section draws together a wide range of questions asked at all the teachings drawn from here. They help to tease out some of the details and clear up subtle and common misunderstandings.

The final part of the book presents *Kindness and Compassion from an Ultimate Perspective*. Ringu Tulku looks here at our fundamental view and how we might refine it, gradually, to see things more clearly. This kind of understanding may be more challenging to grasp and to integrate, but this is the path by which our kindness and compassion can become increasingly informed by deeper and deeper wisdom. Thus they become potentially limitless.

When I was busy bringing up young children, I heard the quote once: 'Children spell love T-I-M-E.' In the welter of advice offered to new parents, this is what stayed with me; I found a truth in it. And there is something about being in the space of an open heart, where love and kindness and compassion are naturally present, that is also about being in a kind of 'heart' time. Time seems so spacious and abundant in a place of kindness, it no longer feels like it is incessantly running forward, or running out. It is just here. We are just here.

So, as you read these teachings, I want to encourage you to invite this quality in, to give time to it. To stop here and there and recollect the simple, real *feeling* of these heart qualities. Now and then perhaps let your breath carry the feeling through your whole being, and beyond: a sense of softening, melting tensions, offering gentleness and acceptance and love. It may nourish you, and gladden your heart, strengthening and ripening these qualities. Which is important, because we will need to be well-versed in these practices to be able to bring them out when things are challenging - when even a few breaths of kindness could transform the situation. I think maybe there is not a moment in life that could not benefit from, and is not deserving of, a breath or two of kindness.

Then, when the challenges come, we can remember, 'This is not a time for waiting until things are better so we can practise. This is the time we have.' And this is the time life really needs us to practise: to soften, to let be, to dare to bear how things are; to allow our hearts to open to things as they are, to open out wider and wider, enough to bear it all. And from that space, we may find we are able to do something to help.

Caught in limited understanding as we inevitably are, many misapprehensions and wrong assumptions arise around kindness and compassion, which we may not even know we have. Ringu Tulku addresses many of these in this text. For example, we often seem to assume that we need to be kind to others *at our own expense*. But this is the good news: Rinpoche reminds us again and again, there is nothing better for ourselves than being kind. It is a 'win - win.' Yet, sometimes, we go about life as if we think we need to somehow 'leap-frog over' ourselves, and send kindness out to others, without it touching ourselves.

Real kindness or compassion, however, need to pass through our own being, suffuse our own cells, soften our own face and be offered to another in an embodied way. We cannot bypass the being we are closest to and most intimately able to influence, ourselves. And we do not have to. We can learn to be kind in an inclusive and embodied way. And this is really important because our misunderstanding (seeing ourselves as a separate 'thing' rather than part of the whole flow of things) can just as easily go the other way and we can become a bit puffed up with misplaced superiority: *'I* am being kind' ... not far behind can easily come, *'I* am so great.' The more we understand Ultimate Bodhicitta, the more these misunderstandings melt away. We are freed from a trap of seeming-separateness and can live more from an awakened heart that knows the true essence of things.

The real power to transform our lives will come from an integrated understanding of both the relative and ultimate levels. We offer this book in the hope that it may contribute to this understanding. As we blend these teachings into our lives, and experientially investigate what Ringu Tulku is pointing us towards, may we come to realise the most profound understanding of kindness. And may it change our lives, and those we share life with, forever.

Mary Dechen Jinpa
On behalf of Bodhicharya Publications
Sikkim, India, January 2017 & Herefordshire, UK, September 2017

The Story of the Cobbler and the Angel

Three most important things about human beings

Buddhist teachings traditionally describe four major sufferings we have to face: birth, old age, sickness and death. The Buddhist view is that most of the trauma we suffer comes from our own birth and death. Birth can be a very traumatic experience, from the point of view of the baby, as well as for the mother. Ageing and sickness can also be very painful. At these times we are helpless and need the help of others. We depend on others.

This depending on others is not something that happens only to one or two people, or only to some people; it happens to all of us. We all face these kinds of suffering and, because of this, all people need help. Nobody is independent. Nobody can do everything on his or her own. This is true, however strong they may be, however arrogant they may be, however educated they may be, however wealthy they may be. We are dependent on other people's kindness and compassion, at those times when we really need them.

One of my favourite stories is from the writings of Tolstoy and is called: *Human beings live by the love of others*. This is true. We live by the love of others. We survive by the love of others. Otherwise we would not exist. Have you heard this story of Tolstoy's? I like this story very much because I think it is very true. It goes something like this:

There was a cobbler, a shoemaker, in Russia, and he was a very kind-hearted man, so that he always gave his customers credit. He would do the work for them and allow them to pay later, which meant he was always poor. Then, Christmas was approaching and it was very cold. But between him and his wife, they had only one coat. So, he decided to go to town and collect all the credit owed him, and buy himself a coat. With the rest of the money, he hoped to bring lots of things for a Christmas celebration, and maybe a special present for his wife.

So, he went to town but he found that everybody he went to see was poor and did not have any money either. He ended up not collecting any funds at all, or buying anything, and so he just went home again. It was late at night by then and, as he passed by a church, he saw a totally naked man who had fallen down just next to the church. At first he thought to himself, 'Ah, I'm not going to get involved with this. It will only get me into trouble.' But then he realised, 'But this man will not survive if he is left like this, because it is December and below freezing. He will certainly die and I can't let him die.' So, the cobbler went and asked the man, 'Where do you come from?' The man did not reply very clearly so the cobbler took off his own coat and put it around the man and brought him home with him.

When he got home, his wife was concerned to find he had brought nothing home with him - except a naked man, another mouth to feed. She was not happy and almost closed the door on both of them, but then she also realised that the man would die without their help. So she said to come in and gave them some hot soup she had prepared. And the man who had been brought to their home, he smiled then. And his smile was so beautiful it was like light radiating and filling the whole house. And everybody felt happy.

They said to him, 'Okay, you can stay here but you have to work; everybody has to work.' The man agreed and the cobbler showed him how to make shoes. He learned immediately and started making very lovely, very special shoes. So the cobbler became a very famous cobbler, due to these lovely shoes, and soon people were bringing him orders from far away places.

One day, a very rich man came in his chariot. He brought a very special kind of leather with him and asked the cobbler if he could make some shoes with it, and that he could guarantee they would last for three years. The cobbler looked at his apprentice and confirmed, yes, they could do that. The rich man said he would pay very highly for that, but they had to last for three years. After the rich man left, again the apprentice man smiled, and filled the whole house with light. He never talked or said anything; he just did what he was told to do.

After two or three days, the cobbler found out that the apprentice had made a grave mistake. He had not made shoes out of the leather the rich man had brought. Instead, he had made a kind of slipper that was usually put on dead people's feet. The cobbler was completely shocked and was about to shout at the apprentice, when there was a knock on the door.

They opened the door and found it was the rich man's driver. He told them, 'We don't need those shoes any more. My master died yesterday. Now we will need those special slippers for his dead body instead.' So they gave him the slippers the apprentice had made.

Some time later, a woman came, with two young girls, needing shoes for the girls. One of the girls had a special need – one of her legs was shorter and one was longer, so she needed shoes made accordingly to fit her. The woman was very nice and very kind to these little children. And again, as soon as they had left, this man smiled and filled the whole house with light. And then he said, 'Now it is time for me to leave.'

The cobbler and his wife were shocked. 'You can't leave, you are such a good worker! And we have become such good friends; you are like a member of the family. But anyway, where is it you are going?'

The man replied, 'Well, actually, I am not a human being. I am an angel.' And then he told them the whole story: He had been sent by God to take the soul of a dying woman, who had given birth to twin girls. The woman was about to die but she was not able to die because she loved the two children so much. She was pleading with the angel not to take her soul, 'If I am gone, who will look after these little children?'

She was crying and pleading and the angel could not take her soul. He went back to God and reported how everything had happened. And God said, 'You don't understand human beings. You have lost your wings. You go down to the human world again and stay there until you learn the three most important things about human beings. Only after you have learned these three most important things, will you get your wings back, and then you can return here.'

And now the angel thought to himself, 'I have learned these three most important things about human beings.' His wings were starting to come out.

'The first thing I learned was when the cobbler brought me into his house and gave me soup. Even if he didn't have anything, he shared what he had. I learned that humans have love in their heart. If they see somebody is really having problems and is suffering, they can open their heart to them. So I saw human beings have love in their hearts. That is the first most important thing I learned about human beings.'

'Then, I learned the second thing about human beings, when this rich and powerful man came to place an order for shoes. I knew that he was going to die that very day - because my friend, another angel, was just behind him, about to take his soul. But the man did not know and was insisting that his shoes should last for three years. So, then, I learned the second thing about human beings: They don't know when they are going to die.'

'Then, I learned the third thing about human beings, when I saw these little girls with their mother. She was not their birth mother; she had adopted them, because their real mother was the woman who died. I had not taken her soul but somebody else did and she died. When she died her body fell on the leg of one of her children and damaged it. So, therefore, one of the girls has a problem with one of her legs. But now I have seen that another woman looked after these children, and gave them as much love and care, as their mother would have. I learned from this another very important thing about human beings: Human beings live by the love of others.'

He had indeed learned the three most important things about human beings. His wings came out fully and he flew back to God, from the chimney top.

Bringing Kindness and Compassion into our Daily Lives

More or less, all of us know that it is helpful to be kind. Especially, we feel it is good for ourselves if somebody is kind to us. We feel that everybody really should be kind to us, and if they are not kind to us, they are bad. But it is not so often that we are kind and compassionate ourselves. We have many different reasons – maybe I should say excuses – for not being kind. But I don't think there is anybody who thinks that, if somebody is not kind to me, it is a good thing. So, we all want that other people are kind to us.

I think this is something it is important for us to understand and reflect upon: that if I want and wish other people to be kind to me, to be helpful and beneficial, to bring a sense of joy and support to me; then maybe it is equally important that I am kind to other people also. I think one of the most important things in daily life is not about knowing this factually, but knowing how to put this into practice; how to use this understanding in our actions and really apply this in our daily life.

Being aware

The Dharma taught by Buddha says that we have only one tool for any kind of practice or training we wish to undertake, whether it is meditation or any other way of cultivating positive things in ourselves, or trying to lessen negative things in us. That tool is sometimes translated into English as 'mindfulness' or 'awareness.' And that mindfulness, or consciousness, or awareness, is simply 'knowing what is happening,' that is awareness. We call it *sheshin* in Tibetan *she* means 'to know' and *shin* means 'continuous' – therefore 'continuously knowing.' There is also the word *tenpa*, which is sometimes translated as 'mindfulness.' *Tenpa* is described in Tibetan sources as 'being aware of what is going on, and then knowing what to do at that time, remembering what to do.' This is the definition of *tenpa*.

So, therefore, to cultivate that *tenpa*, or that mindfulness, is the most important thing. Whether we are on our own, in meditation, or whether we are in communication with somebody else, or we are in the process of doing something, or at any point in the course of our life or in our day, we can learn to be a little bit aware of what is going on. We become aware of what state of mind we are in: 'Am I upset or angry? Negative or hurt? And how am I acting? Am I saying something that is nice or not nice? Am I doing something that is kind or unkind? Something beneficial or something harmful?'

When I realise what I am doing or saying, or feeling or thinking, then, if I feel I am reacting in a way that is not good, not beneficial for myself or others, maybe I am doing something that I would not wish others to do to me; then at that moment I try to stop doing that. And I try to remember what is the right way, the good way, the important way to behave instead. I ask myself how I would like other people to act towards me. This all takes time to describe here, but in reality this process doesn't take any time at all.

If we can get this kind of mindfulness in place, in an on-and-off way, it can bring an awareness of how we are reacting and whether it is the way we would choose to react or not. It is not to say that we could then always be the best; that we would always do the right thing and nothing but that. That is not easy; it is not even possible. But if we can become a little bit conscious, that alone has an effect on how we behave. This is the way to bring kindness into our daily life and not only kindness, but to work with any kind of a training in anything that we wish to cultivate in ourselves. But this has to be based on a very clear understanding, or view, of what is the best or most appropriate way to act.

Clarifying our view

Usually compassion is regarded as a very, very positive and very useful state of mind. It is something that is good for others, but it is also good for us. And this is something I think it is useful to reflect upon. When we reflect in this way, part of the function of that reflection is to clear up some of the misunderstandings and misconceptions about compassion.

I think there are several common misunderstandings and misconceptions about compassion. One of these is about what we mean by the word 'compassion.' I am told the meaning of the word in English is 'suffering together.' This might suggest that if somebody is having a bad time, a painful experience, we should also feel that, we should also suffer as much as that person is suffering. This seems to be part of the understanding of what compassion is, for many people, especially in the West – because many people tell me that 'compassion is a little heavy.'

At first, I didn't understand why people should feel that compassion is heavy. Why should compassion be heavy? Compassion is very nice! But then slowly I came to understand why they felt like this, because if you have to feel all the pain and suffering of everybody, then that is not nice. And I don't know if it would be too useful, either.

From my point of view, when we talk about compassion – *nyingje* in Tibetan or *karuna* in Sanskrit – there is not so much of an idea of suffering together. It is more about wishing to be free from suffering. I think there is a big difference between these two ways of understanding. To feel very painful and suffer as much as other people suffer is a very different idea. Maybe you have to have some understanding, what we call empathy, yes. But if you too much focus on taking the pain and suffering on yourself then it becomes heavy - and it doesn't help too much, either. But if you focus more on the need, and wish, and ways, to change that situation, then it becomes a method; then it really becomes compassion.

Wishing well, warm heartedness

So, the feeling or understanding or experience of compassion is about having a benevolent attitude towards people. It is a feeling of wishing well. His Holiness the Dalai Lama often talks about the expression of compassion being warm heartedness. I think what he means by 'warm heartedness' is exactly this benevolent feeling of wishing well to everybody. When you have this feeling, you feel very good.

I think kindness is something like this also: it is a natural or spontaneous warm hearted feeling. You just naturally wish well. It is not necessarily specifically towards this or that, you just radiate that good will. And when you are feeling like that, your actions, your speech and mannerisms, your expression, all become something that is kind. Something which expresses good heart and good will.

Maybe you don't even do anything very special, but people can feel there is a certain benevolent motivation in you. And when you are feeling like that, you feel good, you don't feel pain or suffering. You feel a natural warmth from within yourself. You don't have a cold feeling inside, but a warm feeling. There is no intention anywhere to harm or cause any trouble. There is not too much self-centeredness and no need to harm people or put people down. There is no feeling of that kind.

So, I think, when one feels kind, one feels very good. I don't think anyone would say, 'I had such a bad time – I was feeling so kind!' So, therefore, it is something that is good for ourselves, as well as for others. And it is something that is good for now and also good in the long run. It is rare that people will say, 'I have this problem now, because I was so kind.' There is no guarantee how other people will react but being kind in itself does not lead to problems.

This is another misunderstanding: people think that if they are kind, people will take advantage of that. They feel that it is not good if they are taken advantage of, so they should not show kindness. I think people *will* take advantage – but people will try to take advantage of you also if you are not kind. And how much people take advantage of you is, I think, up to you. People can ask you to do something and you can *kindly* say 'no.' You can kindly say 'no' or you can kindly say 'yes.' Or you can unkindly say 'no' or you can unkindly say 'yes.' You can always say no, but if you say it in a nice way, it hurts people less.

Choosing your action wisely

It is not that people will not try to take advantage of you, but it is up to you how much you let them do so. If you want to give them a little bit of help, you can let them take advantage a little bit. Or you can let them take advantage a lot, if you want to. It is up to you. I think that is important. Sometimes people think that, 'If I have compassion, then I have to do everything that everybody asks me to do.' They think that, otherwise, they will have broken some rule or something. I don't think this is the case. First of all, you have to see if what they want you to do is useful or not. Will it help that person or not? If somebody asks me to do something, but I know it would not really be helpful, I don't have to do it. Doing it would not be compassionate then. *Not doing* it would be compassionate.

Compassion is not about just doing anything that anyone asks you to do. It is about looking to see if it is good for them if you do it, and whether it is good for yourself, also. And then looking to see if you are *ready* to do that, or not, even if it would be helpful. If you are not ready to do that, then there is no compulsion for you to do it. You can still be compassionate. You can still be kind. I don't think there is any need for you to do everything people ask of you.

You have to be strong to be kind

There is also a widespread misunderstanding that, if somebody is kind, then he or she is not very efficient; he or she cannot handle important responsibilities; he or she becomes weak. I think this is a serious misunderstanding and I think it is causing a lot of damage in society, and in the world. I have heard, myself, people saying, 'This person is not suitable to become the headmistress of a primary school because she is too kind.' And other things like that. They think that if you are kind, you will do everything that people say you should do. Kindness is almost associated with being stupid or being naive.

I do not think this is the case at all. Somebody who is very compassionate can be very intelligent. They can be tough, and also sometimes they can be not that nice. In the Tibetan Kagyu lineage, we have the example of Marpa. He was a great Tibetan teacher, a translator. He went to India and studied Sanskrit and received many teachings and really practised and became highly realised. Then he came back to Tibet and passed on these teachings. He had a particular student called Milarepa, whom he treated really very badly.

Generally, Marpa would do everything he could to help people. He would even try to teach his cats and dogs! He would say to them, 'I went all the way to India and learned all these teachings... listen to me!' And he tried to teach them. And then Milarepa came along, a really dedicated student. But Marpa would not teach him. Instead, he gave him endless troubles. He would make him do all sorts of hard, and ridiculous, things, so that people thought Milarepa was mad or crazy. Even Marpa's own wife became fed up with him, but he would not relent. He just carried on making Milarepa's life difficult. But all the time, he was actually teaching him: he was purifying him and making him ready. And because of that, because of Marpa's hard way of working on him, Milarepa became one of the most advanced and most realised yogis of Tibet. That was Marpa's kindness, his compassion.

This shows how compassion is not necessarily about smiling and being soft. It is about your intention. It is about having a good intention and wishing to be of benefit. It is wanting to bring something good and useful, and being uncompromising in that. Therefore, somebody who is kind and compassionate is also somebody who can, and sometimes should, be strong. This is something people sometimes don't understand. If you are compassionate, you are less self-centered and selfish but that does not mean you are not strong. You can be very courageous. You can be very brave. It actually helps you to be truly altruistic.

A natural quality

Being altruistic is a natural quality, and not only of human beings. Human beings have that quality and it is a very common quality: that you can sacrifice yourself and your own advantages, even your own life, for the sake of others. There are examples all through history of people sacrificing their life - for the sake of their country, for the sake of their people, for the sake of their faith, for the sake of the majority of the people. And that is compassion. We see it not only in human beings, but many animals also have that quality. I am told that the more intelligent the animal, the more they have this capacity to sacrifice themselves for the benefit of others. It is not the stupid animals that do that. It is the intelligent or clever animals that do that.

Compassion is *really* wishing, and having this motivation, to do something that is good for everybody. When you have that motivation in your heart, that kindness in your heart, you feel good; you feel purposeful; you feel well. This is the idea, at least from the Buddhist point of view, but I think it is also the case from many viewpoints. It is healing. The more compassion you feel, the more healing power you have, for yourself and also for others.

The practice of *tonglen*

This is why I have also been asked to say something about the practice of *tonglen* here. Tonglen is all about compassion. It is essentially a meditation practice, which trains us in compassion. It is about healing through compassion. There are two things in the tonglen practice and the first one is that you are working on your negative side.

What is the main source of our fear and anxiety? If I am too afraid or have too much aversion, it causes many problems. But we have a lot of fear and sometimes fear is called aversion – not wanting something, pushing it away. Any experience or anything that I don't want to happen to me or come to me, that is aversion - my not wanting those things to be there. I can also have aversion to things that are *in* me, part of me. I can even have aversion to things that are not there, that are not happening, but *could* be there, *could* happen. As long as we have this aversion, we cannot be okay: we have worries; we have fear; we have anxiety.

Aversion also brings a problem with nice things, something good that you do have. Because you worry that you might lose it. 'I have this wonderful thing... I hope I do not lose it... What must I do so I will not lose it?' This is also aversion. And you will have this fear until you do lose it. That fear does not actually stop until you lose it – or you don't love it any more. And then, if you lose it, you have another problem: how to get it back. Then you have all the struggle of working out what you can do to get it back. So, therefore, when we have too much fear or wanting, it brings a kind of dissatisfaction and pain, which is there all the time.

If we realise this clearly, that as long as I have fear and too much wanting or desire, I will have a problem, then we can ask, 'What is the cure? How can I become free of all this?' There is only one way. I need to face it. I need to face it in such a way that, even if that thing I have aversion to, even if it comes, I can be okay with it. When I can be okay with that, I no longer have aversion to it. When I don't have aversion, I don't have fear. When I don't have fear, it is not a problem.

When I can lessen my fear and aversion, and my clinging and desire, a little bit, that is when my mind can become peaceful. That is when I can truly be in peace. Tonglen is a practice that helps us learn to face those things we are afraid of and have aversion to. And because it is a meditation practice it helps train us in experiencing these things, rather than just intellectually thinking about them.

Dare to breathe in what you fear

We deliberately think about all those things we have aversion to, all the things we don't want, we don't like, that I think will be very bad for me. And I dare to receive them all. I breathe them in. I try to kind of face them, in this way. That is how we train. When we have something that brings a lot of fear in us, how can we learn to lessen that fear other than by facing it? I have to face it.

Sometimes people have a fear of heights. How can they overcome it? First, they need to try going up a little bit high and face that. Then they go a little bit higher and face that. Then gradually a little bit further… Some people have a fear of speaking in public. How to overcome that? They have to *do it*. First, they try talking to two people; then three people; then ten people; until they can talk to a whole group without problem. The more they can do that, the more the fear will dissipate. Because they gradually find it is the same thing to talk to one person or to one hundred people; actually, there is no difference.

This is the concept of tonglen: you dare to receive, and breathe in, what you usually don't want to receive. And you make that a way to purify your own negative side.

Dare to give away what you value

Then you dare to give what you ordinarily don't want to give away. This is the other aspect of the practice of tonglen. You imagine giving out all these nice, good things like happiness and good health. Usually you want to keep all these things for yourself, and you fear losing them. But this only creates a problem for you in the end. So, you exercise on giving them away, at least in your own mind. You feel that feeling on your out-breath, like you are breathing them out.

So, you imagine receiving all these negative things and find nothing goes so wrong; you are still the same. And you imagine giving all these positive things away to other people, and again you find you are still the same. Then, slowly, your fear and clinging can reduce. Because you know how to face your fears.

When you know how to do this – to receive bad things and give away good things, at least in your own mind - your mind can become more spacious. Your experience becomes more spacious. You don't need to be so afraid all the time; so protected all the time. Anyway, we cannot really protect anything. I think this is something very important to consider: Can we really protect anything? Can we really secure anything?

Of course, we can insure things for hundreds of thousands of pounds. But that doesn't really protect me; it doesn't ensure nothing bad will happen to me. What has to happen to me, will happen, whether I am afraid or not. It will happen however afraid I am, or however much I worry. Nobody can say, 'That negative thing did not happen to me, because I worried enough!' I don't think anybody can even think like that. We all know that some bad things that have to happen, will happen, whether we fear them or we don't fear them.

It is the same with good things: they will happen when they have to happen. And good things will also go. And bad things will also go. That is how it is. Our feelings of fear and anxiety do not serve to help. They just torture us and make our lives miserable. When we can let them go a little bit, our lives become much more free, much more joyful, much more successful and much happier. And then we can become kinder, because we are not always afraid of bad things happening.

Being free to be kind

This understanding is the basis. Once we have this understanding, we know that to be kind or compassionate has no negative effect whatsoever, it is only good, only positive. These qualities don't stop me from doing anything positive. They don't prevent me achieving anything I need to achieve. They don't harm me in any way. And they are good for everybody. There cannot be anything better than that.

That is why His Holiness the Dalai Lama sometimes cries when he is teaching about this. When he cries, it is not when he is talking about his difficulties or problems. He always cries when he is talking about Bodhicitta - compassion. He says, 'It is such a wonderful thing, Bodhicitta, it is so wonderful that I have this opportunity to even talk about it.' And then he is so inspired and so moved that he sheds tears, and he cannot speak any more. Because he sees so clearly that it is so useful and so good for myself, and so useful and so good for everybody. And not only that, but the solution to all the problems in the world lies there.

The solution to all the problems in the world

We have all these problems in the world: conflicts, wars, injustice, racism, many different kinds of issues. How can these be changed? Sometimes we may feel that there is no hope of a solution; there is never going to be any change, because we have been in this situation for all of time. The history of human beings is a history of wars.

Sometimes it looks so bleak. But if you look at it in another way, to solve all these problems is not so impossible. If everybody really wanted to solve them, they could be solved in one day.

If everybody decided to be kind to each other today, by tomorrow there would be no more problems. There would be peace on earth, harmony and happiness. Maybe it will never happen because we don't do it. But if we actually did it – if everybody realised that to be kind to each other is really the solution to all the problems - and felt 'I must do it!' - then it could happen. Why not?

If the majority of the people in this world could understand this, then even those people who don't want to be kind would have to *pretend* to be kind. So, if they are pretending to be kind, that would be okay. Just like how some people these days seem to think they need to pretend to be ruthless to be respected. And then what do we do? We elect ruthless people to be in positions of power. And then they do ruthless things to us. And we complain! I think it is important to understand these issues very clearly.

We have to do it

Then it is about how to start. I can only start with myself. It is not something that I can teach other people, to be kind, without being kind myself. It doesn't make any difference if there is a law that everybody has to be kind. There may already be such a law. I don't think there is any law that says you have to be unkind. Or any religion that suggests you should be unkind. Being kind is not about laws or rules, or saying other people should do it. It is about *us doing it*.

If somebody is being unkind to me, I may feel I have some right to be unkind back. In just the same way, people sometimes feel their anger is justified in certain situations. But it is never a solution to play tit-for-tat with these things. It does not change anything. It just escalates any problem. If somebody says something unkind to me, probably the best way to stop the situation getting any worse is actually to be kind to him or her. It can stop the whole process. If anything can, it is that; not being angry or doing something negative.

Sometimes people think that it is very difficult to do something positive in response, when somebody has done something negative toward you. But if we think about what we really want, which drives us to say and do bad things to others and is behind our getting upset, it is that we don't want to be hurt. We don't want something bad to happen to us. The easiest and most effective way to stop these negative things happening is to cut the whole process at the root. If you do something kind and you become friends with the person instead - you honestly try to settle the problem - that is likely to create the situation where any ping-pong back and forth of negativity can stop.

We need to use this understanding to behave and act with awareness and mindfulness. We have so many habitual tendencies, which are totally ingrained in us – we have been afraid and hateful and negative for all time until now – so it will not necessarily change just like that. But that is okay. We need to understand that, yes, we are like that, it is okay, but we can try to minimise it as much as possible. Now we come to our senses, and realise that it is not good, then we can try to stop acting like that.

Negative emotions, letting them go

These negative emotions – hatred, anger, greed – sometimes we think they are very, very strong. They are so strong that when we are under the power of these emotions, we can kill. We can kill hundreds of thousands of people when we are under the power of these negative emotions. We can even get ourselves killed for this end. But, in another way, these emotions are not that strong. Because they change. They change very quickly.

Email shows it very clearly. If you get a negative email and it makes you cross, it is very easy to quickly write an angry message back, isn't it? So, go ahead, write it. But then *don't send it*. Wait until the next day. Then read it again. I will almost guarantee you will not send that mail, because you will have changed. Your anger may have gone, or it will have changed at least. That strong emotion could not maintain itself for even one night. All you needed to do was just delay your reaction. If it can change that quickly, you cannot say it is that strong. And there is no emotion that does not change. It is very important to understand this.

There seems to be much concern, especially in the West, that if you don't express an emotion it will become repressed, and be bad for you – it will make you sick or go mad or crazy or something like that. But what does 'repressed' really mean? Sometimes people say to me, 'When I was a child, I was angry, but my mother didn't let me express that anger so now I have a problem because of that.' 'Such a superpower mother!' I thought to myself. 'She could control somebody's emotions!'

I have a lot of respect and love for my mother, but she does not control my emotions. Even if she told me not to get angry, if I am angry, I am angry. Her order cannot change that. So, I wondered what kind of superpower mother we were talking about here. But then slowly I realised. It is not that the person did not get angry because their mother told them not to. They did get angry but they repressed their anger. They were still angry but they did not express it. They did not hit somebody or break all the plates. But they did keep that emotion.

I think repressing an emotion is holding onto it, keeping that negative emotion and not letting it go, keeping it inside you and locking it in there. I think that is repression. Of course you should not do that! It is not good to keep anything negative. But when you let something go, it goes, and then it is gone. When I let something go, and I don't try to put more fuel on it, then it goes. It often takes a lot of effort to keep

Bringing Kindness and Compassion into our Daily Lives

hold of a negative emotion like anger. You have to keep thinking about it and reminding yourself how bad such-and-such was, how they should not have said such-and-such. You have to keep building a story about it to keep it alive. But this is not necessary. All emotions can go. Only, you have to allow them to.

The one true antidote

So, whatever negative emotion comes, you can learn to let it go. And then compassion comes. Because compassion is the opposite of all these negative emotions; whether we are dealing with anger and hatred and malicious thoughts, or greed and clinging and self-centredness, or jealousy, or arrogance. The opposite of all of these is the same: compassion and kindness. They are the antidote or remedy to almost all of our negative emotions. Once we have kindness and compassion, that will be good for us, because then we have peace in our hearts.

It is one thing to understand these ideas, which both you and I can probably do without any problem. But it is another thing to actually put this into practice. That is what we have to do. This is the challenge.

Questions & Answers

Kindness, compassion and Bodhicitta

Student: What is the difference between kindness and compassion in the way we are talking about them here – *is* there a difference or are they interchangeable? And how do they relate to Bodhicitta?

Rinpoche: When I talk about kindness, I mean having no negative feeling, wishing well and having a benevolent feeling towards everybody. If somebody is asking for advice, we give him or her advice as best we can. If somebody is asking for the way, we show him or her the way. If somebody is asking for help, we try to be nice and at least advise him or her where to get help. Kindness is having no wish to harm anybody. It is a wish to help and wishing well. A kind person is a nice person, a good person. There is nothing negative coming from such a person, no malevolent feeling. It is having a good heart.

Compassion involves a little bit more than that. The word can mean many different things, but, from a Buddhist point of view, compassion is more about wanting to do something to help. It is about wanting to end suffering and pain, really wanting to *do* something. So, being compassionate may not just involve being nice and kind and smiling benevolently, it is a real wish to do something. Somebody who is compassionate may even be a little bit angry or firm. Because, if they see you are doing something that is not good for yourself, they may try all different means to stop you from doing that. Compassion is more about action and is a stronger feeling. In Buddhist texts, compassion is described as wishing to end suffering, wanting to free people from suffering, so it is a little bit deeper than kindness. You may be really doing something to help, even if you don't say so or show it, and your life may be dedicated to helping. That is compassion.

Bodhicitta can be explained in different ways. In a practical sense, Bodhicitta is a commitment. There is Aspiration Bodhicitta and Action

Bodhicitta within this concept and the aspiration part is about making a commitment. It is about wishing to bring all the suffering of all beings to an end, bringing lasting peace and happiness, eventually. And if I cannot do something now towards this, I pray that I will be able to do something in the long run. That would be my destination or ultimate goal. It is committing to this; feeling that it needs to be done and deciding that I would like to do whatever I can towards that. It is a wish but a very strong one, a commitment.

If you make this commitment, and then also take some action towards accomplishing it, that is what we call Action Bodhicitta. Wishing to work for the freedom of all sentient beings from any kind of pain, problems and suffering; in order to do that, I must train myself. Part of that might be doing some meditation. If you meditate with that intention, then it is Action Bodhicitta. Or you might do any kind of practice or action committing to this, a retreat or study or positive action, any of these could be called Action Bodhicitta.

If you have Bodhicitta, then you already have compassion and kindness. All three go together. If you have compassion, you already have some kindness. But you can have kindness and not have the other two. This is how I think it is. So, therefore, kindness is the starting point.

None of these three leads to any problems, for myself or for others, now or in the long run. Sometimes people say, 'Oh, I have been doing too much for others; now I have to look after myself.' This confuses me. Of course, it is good to look after yourself. You can rest if you need to. You should rest; there is nothing wrong with that. But it's not because I have been too compassionate that I need to rest. Maybe physically I cannot do something more for someone, but that does not mean I am being less compassionate. Sometimes it is even better not to do some things that people want you to do. People need to help themselves also. Sometimes it is more helpful to allow people to learn to help themselves, rather than doing everything for them. I think this is often the case, because even if you *can* do something to help, you can't be there all the time. And, otherwise, they will never learn.

Meditating on kindness and facing fear

Student: If you want to meditate on developing kindness and facing fear, what technique is it best to use?

Rinpoche: I think the most important thing is being aware. Awareness is the real meditation and the basic technique of meditation is none other than being aware. First you find somewhere to sit comfortably - but just in a normal way - I don't think you need to sit in too-different a way to usual in order to meditate. Sometimes people try too hard to meditate, trying to be something different from usual. They try to sit in a very particular way, a little bit stiff and rigid perhaps, and hold it kind of tightly. I don't think that's necessary. It is said to be not necessary.

You just be yourself, in a natural way. You relax your body. You relax your mind. You are just being aware. This is being aware just as we are usually, it is not about 'going deep inside' or 'being very concentrated,' it is just about being aware. When we are aware, we know what is going on. We hear things. We see things. We feel things. Emotions come. Thoughts come. We are just aware of our own awareness. And then we allow whatever comes, to come; and go.

If there is a sound, it comes, and then it is gone. Then a thought comes, and it is gone. The moment we say it is there, it is gone. Actually, we cannot hold onto anything. Because, the moment I say it is there, means I have now moved on to a thought, that thought of it having been there. That is the way our mind is. So, you just let go anything that comes up. There is no other way, anyhow. You cannot do anything else really. And when you are like that, you are just being. You can say you are being in the present moment. You are just being aware.

When you are like that, you can't worry. You can only be relaxed, because things are moving and changing all the time but you are not following them. You are just aware of awareness. So, therefore, if a negative emotion comes, or a positive emotion comes, it is just the same – you let it go. You feel peace.

I think if you feel peace, you feel kindness. When your mind is peaceful, naturally you feel joyful, because there is no disturbance. When you feel a little bit joyful, you also feel kind to everybody. You don't feel anger or anything like that. And the more you let it be, the more it becomes like that.

Student: Does it have to be done as a formal meditation or can it just be done during the course of the day?

Rinpoche: In reality, there is nothing called 'formal' or 'informal' meditation. Of course, you can find a nice seat, close the door, turn off your telephone and then sit. But that doesn't mean that you are doing better meditation. Because your mind is still the same. Just because you are sitting like that, it doesn't mean that your mind is not going all over the place - all over the world!

It is a good thing to do, also, because then you are giving a little bit of time to yourself. But actually, it is not about that specific time because – and I find this very interesting to notice – when we do something, not only meditation, but anything that we do, I find that we are always doing it, *to finish it*. We are always feeling, 'Ah, now I am doing this...' with a certain kind of expectation that I am getting through it, I am finishing it. We are not doing anything with a feeling of relaxing in it, or enjoying it. We are always *finishing* it. So, when you start to meditate, you put a clock there and say, 'Right, now I have to meditate for ten minutes...' and you sit... until, 'Ah, now I am done!' - Did you really do any meditation? Or were you just waiting to finish ten minutes?

This is true, not only for meditation, but for everything we do. We *prepare* to live all the time. We don't really live our life properly. We prepare to enjoy our life. We never enjoy anything. We are always thinking, 'After this...after this...' I think that is a problem with us.

So, therefore, when you are meditating, it doesn't matter how much time you spend on it or whether it is formal or informal; when you are doing it, just *do* that. That is the important thing. Even if it is only for a few seconds. You are just aware of yourself and you relax, whatever is happening. You let things be. You let things go.

Letting go doesn't mean trying to push away. Letting go is just letting be. When you realise something is there, it is already gone, in a way. So, you can just relax. I think this is very useful to do - for life. Even in the busiest times, you can relax. You *need* to relax actually, if you are really busy. If you feel stressed, it is not really useful. It stops you doing anything fruitful. You are just caught up feeling uptight. Instead, you need to breathe out, breathe in, deeply. You can still do whatever you have to do but you can be relaxed. If you do that, I think that is real practice, because then you are actually working on yourself.

Connecting with tonglen practice

Student: I first learned tonglen practice through listening to Pema Chödrön's teachings. The way that she taught it was that, when you breathe in, you become aware of an uncomfortable feeling of your own and then you think of all the other people who may also feel like that. I'm good at the first bit, of feeling an uncomfortable feeling, but then when I try to think about other people who also might feel like that, I get a bit lost and find it hard to connect with that. Because I think, 'So many people are in such a worse situation than myself, I am just a rich Westerner, who am I to complain?' So, then, I find it hard to connect with other people who I imagine might feel the same as me.

Rinpoche: Whether someone is a Westerner or not, it is all the same, people have the same way of feeling, no? Or do 'Westerners' have a different way of feeling?

Student: Ah, no, of course not. What I meant is that I have all these good things – good health, free health care, a secure job, proper wages, good material things, a good standard of life – how can I feel sad about anything when I have all this?

Rinpoche: Ah, that has nothing to do with it. Yes, you have all those things and so you are very lucky. That is good. But you can think about those people who don't have all that. You are having all these good things, and still you have problems. So, those people who don't have any of those things, how many more problems would they have?

Student: So, then, how can I complain?

Rinpoche: The problem is not about complaining. Tonglen is not about complaining. Tonglen is about *giving*; and *facing*. Now, you say you have all these good things. If you were in the same way as all those people who have none of these things and then, on top of that, you were very sick and in pain, how would you feel? You would not be happy. So, then, do you want those people to be free of that too?

Student: Yes, of course!

Rinpoche: Yes, that is *exactly* what you want. So, then, that is the practice. You wish them to be free of all these negative feelings, and then you feel that you kind of take on – this is only a *mental* exercise – you feel that all these negative feelings and negative things they have, including the reasons and causes and conditions of them, you kind of 'take them off' the other people and take them into you and then you purify them. And then all those nice things you have, more than just the insurance and the job, also the joy and compassion and feeling of complete peace, you feel that you give that out to them. And you feel that everybody in the whole universe feels free of all negative feeling and has this wonderful sense of kindness, joy, peace and happiness. You feel that.

Questions & Answers 31

When you feel that everybody is like that, actually, who is feeling that? You are feeling that. So, you are exercising that feeling. You are reducing your negative feeling and increasing your positive feeling. That is the practice. The more you do that, the more it affects you. It affects you the most, that is the whole point, and then it may also affect other people.

Helping ourselves, and helping others, through practice

Student: Sometimes I have the impression with tonglen practice, that it can help the person you are directing it towards, and then sometimes I realise that, actually, what it is about is working on ourselves. So, I was wondering, how then does it affect the other person or other people?

And then I thought that maybe the way it works is that when you're in a situation or some kind of relationship or friendship with someone – some kind of attitude in the world with one person or a group of people – there can be a kind of dynamic or situation that goes on and on and that can get quite locked. But then if one person in that dynamic can change their attitude, then the whole thing can change. So, I wonder if there is an element of that happening in tonglen? Like, if you can work on yourself and change yourself, it can automatically change a whole situation.

Rinpoche: I think it is like this: as you say, this kind of practice affects yourself first and most of all, because it is a practice that *you* do. If you do it from your heart, I think it definitely has an effect on you. Because you are generating compassion and you are working on letting go of your aversion and attachment and things like that. So, it must have some effect on you.

Now, how much it helps others, maybe that depends on lots of other conditions. Maybe it depends also on how highly trained and developed you are, as the person who is doing the practice. Maybe it also depends on other circumstances. Any situation or dynamic depends on many different kinds of things, many karmic conditions and so on. Also, if you are doing tonglen for a specific other person, whether it helps them or not will depend on what kind of connection they have with you – and how deep the trouble is, that that person is in – and many other things.

So, I think it is possible that the practice can have more effect sometimes or less effect other times. It is also possible that it has an effect but you don't see it. And sometimes there is no effect. It will depend on many things, including the strength and capacity of the practitioner, and the many karmic conditions of the situation.

There is a story from my own childhood, about Jamgon Kongtrul of Shechen: my parents fully believed that he took on my pain. Once, when I was a baby, I was in great pain and had not slept for several days and nights, and they thought I was almost dying. So, at last my father went to ask Jamgon Kongtrul to come and do something. He came very urgently. He had been doing a big practice in a particular place, but he left immediately, finishing the practice while travelling. He had to cross a big river by boat, so he was doing his practice on the boat. And then he arrived at my house. And when he arrived, he immediately got sick.

He got really sick, turning red and blue, and was in a lot of pain. He didn't do anything else, but just went to bed. And, almost at that same time, I finally went to sleep. The next morning, when he woke up, he was completely okay. And he asked them to bring the baby – that was me. He didn't say anything about curing me, or anything like that, but he did say, 'This baby is my monk now. He is not a monk of Shechen monastery, or any monastery, he is just my personal monk.' And so I became a monk at that time. My parents completely believed that he took on my illness.

But there is another example, from later on, when the Chinese came to Tibet and many negative things were happening, and someone asked him to do some practice to change the situation. And he said, 'Well, this is something it is not possible to change. If I concentrate on this, I almost get suffocated like I am dying. Something here cannot be changed; the karma is very strong. It is not something that is within my capacity to change.' So, maybe there are some situations that it is not possible to change, or maybe not possible to have a big or strong effect on.

I once met Dr. Emoto, 'the water man.' He was a Japanese research scientist who did a lot of research into water and what influences its structure and behaviour. He exposed water to many different conditions and showed that pure intention and prayers and positive thinking can have a beneficial or harmonising effect on the crystals that form. Different conditions influence the shapes and patterns that the water molecules form. So, he supposes from this, that since the human body is made up of around 60% water, maybe it is possible that you can have a positive effect on human beings through prayer and positive thoughts. Also, the world is made up of a majority of water too, so maybe if many people were to send positive thoughts and prayers towards something, it could have an effect.

'Justified anger'

Student: People often seem to feel that their anger is justified, like you were saying, which seems to stop them moving on or letting it go. Quite a lot of people hold on to issues from the past, in this way, and use these issues to continually be angry in the present - and probably in the future too! What do you attribute this to? And how can it be stopped? How can it be cut at the root?

Rinpoche: I think this is the basic problem - it is what we call *ignorance* - we don't know how to do that, how to stop it. It is like an addiction. We have been reacting like this over and over again, because we didn't know anything better, we didn't know any better way of reacting. So, we did this again and again and then it became our habitual tendency, our addiction. Then it is very difficult to change. Every addiction is like that. Even if you don't want to do something, it is very difficult to stop.

So, therefore, this is why we need to first understand very clearly that this is not the way. This is not good; it is not useful. And then we need to become more mindful, become aware again and again, so that in every moment we try to experience this issue a little bit differently. If we can do that, then, maybe slowly, it can probably change. It is not something we can change straight away, like any negative habit. But over time, we can do that. That is the idea.

Compassion for people it is hard to feel compassion for

Student: How can we apply compassion to those who won't accept it; like religious fanatics, for instance?

Rinpoche: I think it is not about accepting or not accepting compassion. The compassion is my feeling. Their accepting or not accepting it, is another thing. If I have compassion, then I change myself. But then, sometimes it is easier for us to feel compassion towards some people and not others.

For example, we may easily feel compassion towards people who have a worse situation than ourselves, compared to people who have a better situation than ourselves. Sometimes people have that experience. But actually, people who have a better situation than you also have their own problems. So, there is no reason why you should not feel compassion towards them.

Sometimes, people find it easier to feel compassion for people who are nice and good and positive, but find it very hard to feel compassion for people who are doing very bad things, negative things. To have compassion for those people who are doing bad things does not mean that what they are doing is right. It does not mean that you approve of it. Compassion is needed because these people are very unfortunate; these people are very misguided. They are doing something that is very harmful to other people but it is also very harmful to themselves. They are not doing something useful or that is bringing good things and happiness to themselves. They are doing something that is bringing lots of problems for themselves also. So, therefore, you can be compassionate.

Compassion does not say, 'Okay, I will let them do all these negative things.' If somebody is doing negative things, I think you should try to stop them if you can, because if you can stop them, that will be much better for them. If I try to stop them, it is not because I hate them, it is because I have compassion for them. This is important to differentiate – your compassion and your action. I have compassion for them but that does not mean I let them do whatever they want.

I was actually quite impressed by an answer His Holiness Karmapa gave to a question about this. One time when I was translating for His Holiness, the present Karmapa, the 17th Karmapa, when he was quite young; somebody asked him, 'If somebody slaps you on your cheek, should you turn the other cheek, or not?' Many times I have also been asked this question. I didn't know exactly what to answer but then I was quite moved by his answer.

Karmapa said, 'When people turn the other cheek, they are thinking of their own positive situation, you could say their own positive karma. They don't want to do anything to jeopardise that. So, they just turn their other cheek and let the person slap them. But they are not thinking about the karma of the person who is doing that.

Because he or she is doing something wrong and they are just letting them. They are almost supporting the action. If they were thinking about the karma of the person who was slapping them, then maybe they would stop them.'

I thought this was a useful way of thinking about it. You stop the bad action, not because you are angry, but because you are compassionate. If you are compassionate, you should not allow bad things to go ahead.

Wrathful compassion

Student: Can you say something about wrathful compassion?

Rinpoche: Wrathful compassion is just the same as what we have been talking about. The only thing is you act in a forceful or powerful way. Maybe you do something that doesn't *look* that nice and kind - it looks a little bit rough and tough - but it is actually done with a deeply beneficial motivation; for example, thinking about the other person, who may be doing something wrong.

Student: Is it related to anger, or is it something different?

Rinpoche: It is not about being angry; it is just about the way in which you act. Your action is forceful rather than all 'nicey-nice.'

Taking a vow to become a Bodhisattva

Student: How do you go about taking the Bodhisattva Vow? How do you prepare for it and what is the process of taking it?

Rinpoche: The Bodhisattva Vow is a kind of formal way of making a commitment that you wish to generate the motivation of Bodhicitta and become a Bodhisattva. You just need to understand a little bit about that and, if you feel you want to be a Bodhisattva, you want to generate Bodhicitta, then you just take the vow. Don't think too much about it!

Generally, for good things you want to do, you don't need to think too much. If you are about to do a bad thing, then think! But if you want to do a positive thing, just do it. I think that is the best approach.

To take the Bodhisattva Vow is to become a Bodhisattva. You can take it in front of a person, in front of a Lama. Or you can just take it by yourself. You can imagine all the Buddhas and Bodhisattvas, all the Enlightened Beings, are there in front of you and you just make the vow. You can take it in a shrine room where there is a nice representation of the Buddha, you can take it in front of that. But the main thing is yourself – you yourself make the vow that:

> 'As the Buddhas and the Enlightened Beings of the past have generated the motivation of Bodhicitta, and then trained on the path of the Bodhisattva, in order to benefit all beings; I, too, would like to generate Bodhicitta and train myself on the Bodhisattva path, step by step and gradually.'

You just say that in your heart, or in your own voice three times, and the vow is taken. You become a Bodhisattva – with shining armour! In fact, it is recommended that you take some kind of a Bodhisattva vow regularly, even every day. Because it is about making an aspiration, which we need to affirm and reaffirm. Every time you take the vow it is like a purification.

Expecting gratitude

Student: Quite often we do things to help people, thinking we have a pure motivation but then, when they don't thank us, we become upset and feel unappreciated. Does this show us that our motivation was not a hundred percent pure?

Rinpoche: It is possible to have a pure motivation. But it is also possible, and very common, to have a kind of 'mixed-up' motivation. We are samsaric beings, so we are likely to have a bit of our own agenda mixed up in things. We don't have to feel bad about that, it is only natural; but we do need to see if that is the case and correct it wherever we can.

Then, another thing, which is also extremely important, is that, even if you do have a good motivation and even if you do something really good for others, it is likely that nobody will appreciate you for it! I think it is very important to know, right from the beginning, that it is *most likely* that nobody will appreciate you and nobody will thank you. Otherwise you are in trouble. Because you will be wondering, 'Okay, when is the appreciation coming? When are they coming with bouquets of flowers?' And, most of the time, they will not be coming at all.

'Mixed-up' motivation

Student: I think I have an example of how an impure motivation might affect things. Some years ago, I wanted to do something nice for somebody, but I also had some kind of 'greediness' of wanting to be liked, which I did not admit to myself at the time. So, I did the helpful thing and over the years continued to give in that way, but I found I was building up resentment at the same time. If I had been clearer in my mind, through practising meditation, I might have been able to prevent harming myself and harming the other person.

Rinpoche: Yes, I agree, this is very important. Sometimes, we think we are doing something good but we don't even recognise that there are other intentions behind what we are doing. We get upset because of those other intentions, feeling we are not appreciated and so on. Then we think it is because we have been too kind, but actually it is not because we are too kind. It is because we have other motivations hiding behind the ones we are aware of.

Healing yourself before helping others?

Student: If you have experienced a lot of suffering or loss yourself, as a child or later, before you do any practice like tonglen or anything like that, is it not important that you should acknowledge this and be kind to yourself and really try to heal this, before you take on such practices to help others? Is it not a problem if you try and ignore your suffering and help others before that healing process has taken place?

Rinpoche: Actually, I have been thinking a lot about this. Lots of people suffer a lot – in their childhood, in their youth, in life. What I see is that the different ways of looking at this suffering can make a lot of difference. But I don't really know if there is something called, 'Now I heal this,' and it is healed. How do I heal the suffering?

Student: By acknowledging what has happened? By recognising it.

Rinpoche: But recognising such suffering is not very difficult - if you have had lots of problems and suffering, you know it is there.

Student: By being kind?

Rinpoche: But you can be kind anyway, whether you have experienced lots of suffering or not. Sometimes I see it like this: When somebody goes through a very difficult time, whatever kind of an experience it is, a very painful or traumatic experience, maybe you would call it abuse; when you go through that, there are two ways of looking at it, yourself.

One is, 'Oh, I have gone through a very, very difficult time, a very painful time, but then, thank goodness, it is over now.' Or something like that. When you can say that, then I think you can be healed from it. You can get strength from what happened. Something happened; it was very bad; but you got through it and you could leave it behind.

But sometimes, people identify with it too much. They go through a difficult or painful time and they say or feel, 'Oh, I am the one who had this trauma.' And sometimes other people assist with this, saying, 'Oh, you are the one who had this difficult time. You are the one who had this trauma happen to you; you are the one who had this pain.' And then the person says, 'Yes, I am the one who had this trauma.' They identify with it so much so that they can never leave it, because it has become their identity.

In reality, we go through all different kinds of times in life: bad times, good times, traumatic times and painful times. They happen and we go through them. We don't need to get stuck at one point. If you identify too strongly with one particular experience, you get stuck there, and once you have identified so strongly with something, I think there may be almost no way to get rid of it.

But if we say, 'This is life.' Life is changing. It is moving; it is happening; it is transforming. Today is nice; tomorrow is not nice; the next day is better. Life is full of changes. Good things happen in life. Bad things happen in life. Some bad things you could never have imagined can happen. Some good things that you never imagined can happen, also. That is life. Life is like that.

So, good things also happen in life but we don't tend to identify with them in the same way. 'I am that good thing!' - we hardly ever say that. Do you say that? I have not yet met one person who does. But we could do, logically. We could say, 'I am the one who...went for a picnic!' We could identify with all sorts of positive things in our lives.

Actually, something did happen to me like that, something I am a little bit proud of, when I was a young boy. There was a great Indian President called Sarvepalli Radhakrishnan, who was a learned philosopher and a very great man. His birthday was 5th September and this day is declared as Teacher's Day in India. He was indeed a very great teacher. And, when I was just ten years old, I learnt the Indian national anthem from him, himself!

At the time of this story, I was living at the Young Lamas' Home School in Dalhousie and we would often be invited to go and meet dignitaries and so forth. We went to Delhi to meet the Indian President and, for the meeting, we had to learn the Indian national anthem. But I didn't learn it very well - I was the smallest and they didn't take much interest in me, so no one noticed. I was only ten or eleven years old and everybody else was in their twenties. So, they all learned it, and we went to Delhi.

There was a big, nice lawn; we all lined up there and after some time the President arrived, wearing thick glasses and a turban and with many bodyguards. So, we started to sing the national anthem, while he walked along the line. Then he came to me, and as he was listening to me, my voice got smaller and smaller... Then he sat down in front of me. And, to my very greatest shock, he said, 'Let us sing it again!'

So, we sang it again. And when we had finished, he said, 'Let us sing it *again*!' Three times we sang it. And I memorised it then in such a way that I never, ever forgot it after that! So, I learned the national anthem of India from *the* Indian President. I am a little bit proud of that.

Actually, I had a very good time while at the Young Lamas' Home School. I have also had very bad times. But I usually remember the good times. It's better like that, no? In a lifetime lots of things happen, good things, bad things, all sorts of things. That's the main thing to understand. Lots of good things can happen in life. Lots of bad things can happen. Death happens also. The story of Gautami, from Buddha's time, is a good example.

The story of the woman who lost her son

This young woman, Gautami, had a very loving son and they were very happy but then, when he was only eight years old, he suddenly died. She could not accept it, and was running to everybody saying, 'This can't be happening! Please do something!' Everybody was passing her on to someone else until finally someone said, 'Go and see Buddha. He is highly realised and very wise. Maybe he can help you.' So, she went to see Buddha and asked him, 'Please can you help me. My son has passed away. But it can't be like this. Please can you revive him or something? Bring back his life.'

Buddha said, 'Okay, but first you have to do something.' She was happy to do anything so he said, 'Bring me first a handful of sesame seeds.' She was about to run off to do so, when he said, 'No, no, there is a condition: Bring me a handful of sesame seeds, collected from a family in which nobody has died. And then I will revive your son.'

So, she immediately ran to the first family she came to and asked for some sesame seeds. They were about to go and fetch some for her when she asked, 'First though, has anyone died in your family?'

'Yes,' they said. 'My father died and then also my mother died.'

She asked other families: 'My grandfather died.' 'My grandmother died.' 'My sister died.' 'My brother died.' 'My child died.' She went through the whole city and could not find a single family in which nobody had died.

And then she understood. Death is imminent and everybody dies. And there is no rule that says: first old people die and then young people die. Old people die. Young people die. Middle-aged people die. Children die. 'This is not only something happening to me,' she realised. 'It happens to everybody. This is a fact of life.'

When she realised this, she went and cremated her child and then went back to Buddha. Buddha asked, 'Where are the sesame seeds?'

'I don't have any sesame seeds. I have cremated my child. Now I am here to follow you and study the Dharma.' So, she became a student of the Buddha. She practised and I think she became the first female Arhat, the first female Enlightened Being, of that time.

This is the important thing to realise: painful and traumatic things happen to lots of people, and to everybody in one sense or another. The more you understand that this is something that is experienced by many people; that it is not something extraordinary, it is almost normal in this world; then the more this can help you accept your own traumas: 'There *is* lots of suffering. It is not a good thing but it happens. Lots of people have this kind of suffering. It is not something extraordinary that is happening only to me.' Then you can accept it a little bit more deeply.

Once you can accept this, it brings more compassion. Because you realise that lots of people are suffering in the same way. 'And those people who are suffering, are suffering *as much as I am*.' This opens your heart to others. You feel how you are not the only one who is suffering, so you are no longer locked into *your own* suffering. Suffering is everywhere. That brings a sense of compassion and opens your heart to other people also. I think that is the starting point of compassion towards others.

Renunciation, attachment and love

Student: Can you say a bit about renunciation and attachment, from the Buddhist point of view, in relation to loving our families and children?

Rinpoche: Renunciation is knowing what the causes of suffering and pain and problems are, and what the causes of our freedom from these are; and then making effort to let go of those causes and conditions that lead to suffering. Making a decision to train ourselves on letting go of those is renunciation. And then, again and again, we have to look in our heart and see if we are still on track with this or not. Renunciation is not about leaving any thing or any place or any people; it is about giving up our attachments and aversions to things and within relationships. It is about not being bound by attachment and aversion in our own mind.

But people often misunderstand this idea. I met one person who said to me, 'I don't want to study Buddhism or practise Dharma because Dharma says you have to be free from attachment but I have lots of attachment to my children.' This is a misunderstanding. Dharma always teaches: *the most important thing is compassion and wisdom, or love and wisdom.* Compassion is therefore the most important thing to cultivate in Dharma, or in Buddhism; it is the most important thing not to reject. I also met one person who had been emotionally cold to his wife and children for many years because he thought that was necessary for practising Dharma. But this is very wrong. We need to love.

Actually, love and attachment are two very different things. In the samsaric state of mind, they are very mixed up, but actually they are completely different. Real love is selfless. If your child were suffering and you would rather suffer instead of them, that is true love. Attachment is different. Attachment is all about 'I.' Attachment kind of love is very conditional. It is saying, 'I love you, as long as you love me, and you do what I want. If you don't, I hate you.' This kind of love can turn into hatred in no time at all. That is not real love. That is attachment.

Real love is not about me, it is about the other person. Whatever that person is doing, it does not matter, I still love them. It is unconditional. And this is the kind of love that is encouraged by Dharma, and not only to one person but to everybody. Not a conditional love but a real wishing well. The wellbeing of the person you love is what is so important. If it is my wellbeing I am more concerned about, that is attachment.

So, therefore, when we talk about not being attached, we are talking about a real or true love. A much better kind of love. Attachment is something that can never be fulfilled. That is the whole point. We want something; then we want something else. But happiness and fulfilment have to come from within.

Choices

Student: I understand we can increase our compassion by working with our ill will. Sometimes I can clearly see that I have a choice: If a feeling of ill will comes up, I can either go with it, follow it, or I can decide not to. But other times I feel like I don't have a choice – about what my actions are. So they may not be 'wholesome' then. My question is: do we just work with the times we can see, and then our perception will gradually become clearer, like muddy water settling? Because I feel I get swept away sometimes and I don't even see what my thoughts are, until I come out the other side of them and realise, 'I've been there again.'

Rinpoche: Yes, I think we have to work with what we can see. There is no other way. Because sometimes we are just carried away with our emotions and reactions. But then afterwards, what then? If you can see beforehand that this emotion is coming, or this reaction is coming, and you can see, 'I should not react like this; I should react like that.' Then you have a choice and then you can choose the better option. It is not always the case that you *can* choose the better option, sometimes you cannot. But you can try to choose the better one.

But sometimes, you have already done something; you have said something or done something or something has happened. It was just how you reacted at the time and it is now too late to alter. But, later on, you come to see that you should not have reacted like that. The way you reacted was not so great. It was not very wise. It was not so good for others or for yourself. But then, also, you have a choice. You can think, 'I have done what I have done but, now, how I keep it, how I hold it in my emotions, there I have a choice.' I have a choice whether to hold onto my reaction or emotion or whether to let go of that kind of reaction or emotion. This is another choice.

There are always many different levels of such choices. So, even if you could not help but react in a way that was not good, then later on, if you do not hold onto that, that is also a great practice. Even how long you hold onto it, or how strongly you hold onto it, all these things make a difference. Sometimes, I cannot help but that I am upset, I am angry; but then I understand that it is not good for me to become hateful. So, I manage to remain just angry and do not let myself become hateful. Or sometimes I might feel angry but I manage to prevent myself from acting on it, or doing anything that might actively harm others. There are many levels. We need to work at wherever we are. Even if we can make a little improvement, at whatever level we are at, that is a good thing.

Helping the elderly

Student: I am interested to know if you have any ideas or recommendations for me, to help my ninety-three-year old mother accept that she is the age she is, with the limitations that she has. She is so angry that she has reached the age of ninety-three, with the physical and visual limitations it has brought her, that she is very difficult to be around. I do try, in whatever way I can, to encourage her and make her feel that she is a valued person and, really, has had a wonderful life. But I just wondered if you had any tips for me?

Rinpoche: What I have found is that, as you become older and older, you become like a child. We have two childhoods; one is the 'beginning childhood' and one is the 'end childhood.' The end childhood is very difficult. Because when you are in the beginning childhood, it gets better, but when you are in the end childhood, it doesn't - it gets worse! It never gets better, so it is very difficult. Also, you cannot teach people in the end childhood. In the beginning childhood, you can teach them. But in the end childhood, you cannot, because they already know much better than you do, or at least they think they do.

So, I think it is difficult. Of course, you can try to remind them of good ways of looking at things, but whether they accept them or not is another matter. Usually if someone has been a certain way all their life, it is not easy to change at this stage. If you have not changed something all your life, now at ninety-three years old, to change is kind of a 'tall order.' So, there may not be that much we can do. I think the main thing is to be kind. Whatever they think, try to support that and encourage them. Anyway, we don't have too much choice here. I usually agree with everything they say. There is no use in disagreeing. What would be the use?

The main thing is that they can *feel* and if you can bring a loving, caring feeling to them, they can feel that. That, I think, is very helpful – at any age. Even people with Alzheimer's or who have advanced dementia, they can still feel this. I know a nurse in Norway who looks after people in an old people's home, and she says that there are lots of people there who don't remember anything, who are completely 'lost.' But she comes in and tries to be nice to them; she brings them nice food, chocolates and things like that. Even though they don't remember her name or anything, as soon as they hear her voice, they become alert and happy, even joyful. They *feel* her attitude. I think that is the important thing: the heart feeling.

A purposeful life

Student: What is the purpose of living so long, from the Buddhist point of view, if all your independence and your faculties are taken away from you?

Rinpoche: I don't know! Everybody wants to live long, no? People are afraid of dying. Even at the age of ninety-three…ninety-four…ninety-five, they would almost do anything to survive. They might complain, 'Why am I not dying?' but most people still want to live.

There is nothing called the 'Buddhist point of view' of this. Some people live long. Some people live short. There is no purpose in living short. There is no purpose in living long. But people do. There is nothing called 'this is the purpose.' We have to *make* the purpose. I have to make the purpose of my own life. There is nothing called 'this is the purpose of your life,' given by somebody else.

And I think we do need to make our lives purposeful, whether long or short. It is not up to us whether we live long or short; we have no choice. Some people have a long life, and may be healthy too. Some people have a long life but may be very unhealthy or sick. Some people have a short life. These things are not in our control. Of course, we can try and do whatever we can. People go on health drives, eating good food etc. Although I often see people eating very bad food... doing very hard work ... and yet hoping to live longer! It is the case that sometimes we can do something to support our health and longevity but sometimes it does not work.

I think the important thing is that, when we are dying and we look back at our life, whether we feel there was some purpose in our life or not depends on whether we did something that really benefitted people. If I had done something that benefitted some people, or helped society or the world in some way, however small or little it was, then I think I would feel that my life was not totally useless. But if I found that I had done nothing; I just survived and did nothing to help anybody or make any difference to anybody, then I think I might feel my life was useless. So, by trying to do something that is useful or helpful for some people in some way, I think that is the way of making a purpose for our life.

'Compassion fatigue' and empathy

Student: What about 'compassion fatigue' or 'burn out?'

Rinpoche: How we are and how we experience things depends on how our mind is focused. If my mind is focused on something positive, wonderful and good, something that gives us satisfaction, happiness, joy and peace, then we feel that way. Whether I feel calm, satisfied and at peace, or whether I feel tense and distressed, depends on how, or where, my mind is. If I focus my mind on kindness and compassion and possibilities of good things, on positive qualities, then I can become happy and joyful; kind, compassionate and peaceful. If I focus on all the negative things that are going on in the world and that could go on, then I can become very unhappy and unsettled.

It is very important to understand this. It is not about what is going on; it is about how I focus. Good things are going on all the time; bad things are going on all the time. There has been lots of suffering going on in the world, all the time, since the beginning of samsara. And it will continue till the end of samsara, with all these problems and difficulties. That is not to say we should not try to understand this suffering. It is to say that we should focus on it in another way.

In the summer of 2016, I attended a conference with His Holiness the Dalai Lama in Strasbourg, where he was participating in a dialogue with scientists at the University of Strasbourg. There were many scientists there, presenting their research and so forth. One scientist, an eminent woman neuroscientist from Germany, presented some very interesting findings. She has been conducting a lot of research into compassion, including a big project with 2000 participants and 300 research scholars. They found that when people have empathy for others, it could go two ways. Empathy can bring stress and burn out, and depression. Or empathy can bring good things, like compassion, strength and courage.

Her view, from her research, was that it depended on how you focused that empathy. She said that, if you feel there are lots of people suffering and they have such great problems, and you 'take it upon yourself' and feel bad about that; then it can bring burn out and depression and things like that. Because you focused on yourself, you kind of took it on yourself.

But, in the same way, if you feel that there are problems and suffering and pain, but then, instead of brooding on it or feeling that pain in yourself, you think, 'What can I do to change it?' You kind of focus 'outside' of yourself. Then it becomes compassion. Then you don't get burnt out. You don't become depressed. You become more courageous and strong and compassionate.

She said there was a very big difference between these two responses. Of course, empathy, or feeling with others, is necessary to have compassion. But it is interesting to note that empathy does not always result in feeling in a good way. We need to understand and feel the suffering and pain and problems of other people but it is not helpful to dwell negatively on them. There is a lot of suffering, that is there and it has been there for a long time. But it needs to be changed and it *can* be changed. It might not be easy but it can be changed. So, I need to do something about it. And whatever I can do, I should do. If I can do a little bit, that much better. I can't necessarily change everything just like that, now. But eventually maybe I can help to.

When your way of looking becomes like that, then empathy does not become a source of frustration or burn out or depression. It brings courage and determination. That is where the attitude of the Bodhisattva comes from. This is the attitude of the Bodhisattva. There is lots of pain and suffering and problems in the world, and not only in this world but wherever there are beings, whatever kind of beings they may be. Wherever beings are, if they are in the samsaric state of mind, they will suffer. So, therefore, this has to change; they should not suffer. But it is not the case that someone can just wave a magic wand and all beings are free from suffering. It takes time, because in the end people have to do it themselves, because it is about our frame of mind, whether we suffer or not.

So, therefore, the Bodhisattva tries to work towards that, towards every being becoming free from all suffering. To do so, it is necessary to have some idea how that is possible: By changing something within, realising something within; by working on ourselves we can certainly become happier and suffer less. That we all know. So, if I can become a little bit better, then maybe I can become better and better still, until I am completely free from all suffering and pain and problems. If I can become like that then everybody can become like that. If one person can do it, then another person can do it; then everybody can do it. And they should do it.

So, why didn't everybody become free of suffering already? Because they didn't know it was possible, they didn't know that they could do it. Even ourselves, we all want to be free from suffering and pain and problems. The world wants to become better. But sometimes, because we don't know how to do this, we can also become worse, create more suffering for ourselves.

It is true that, in many ways, the world has become better in the last one hundred years, but we have also created a lot of problems. Someone said we have created a situation where all the life forms on earth may become extinct in the future. And we have created so many weapons now, that we could destroy the world many times over. Yet, we did this in order to 'protect ourselves!'

His Holiness the Dalai Lama says he thinks the world has become better. He asked the Queen Mother of England, who has since passed away, about this, when he met her when she was around one hundred years old. He asked her, 'You have lived over one century and are one of the longest lived people, let alone being one of the longest lived members of the monarchy. You have seen many things. Tell me, very frankly, what do you think? Has the world become better or worse over your lifetime?'

He said that she replied, without any hesitation, 'No, no, it has become much better now!' She was very confident and very clear. 'It has become much better now because, when I was young, things like equality and human rights were not even thought of. We did not even have the *concept* of human rights. Now we are talking about these things and fighting for human rights. Many things we are talking about and discussing nowadays were not even concepts before. Many things have developed and are much better.'

Maybe there are many things which can be improved, and which *should* be improved, but there are also many things which are much better. The Bodhisattva's attitude therefore needs to be a very long-term attitude. Compassion has a very long-term view. That is why Shantideva's prayer says,

> *'As long as space remains,*
> *As long as sentient beings endure,*
> *So may I, too, remain*
> *And dispel the miseries of the world.'*

This is the Bodhisattva's prayer and intention: 'As long as there are beings in the world suffering, may I always be there to help and transform suffering.' When you have that kind of attitude, you are not thinking too much about yourself or how you yourself are feeling. Which means you can't be frustrated or burnt out or anything like that. This is the importance of focusing our mind on an ideal like that of the Bodhisattva.

Relative and Ultimate Bodhicitta

Student: It seems the Buddhadharma is spoken of in two ways - there is the relative, like in the Lojong teachings [Mind Training]. These talk about compassion that we can develop, over time, Relative Bodhicitta. But is there another aspect of compassion, which is to do with the nature of things? - An 'Absolute' level of compassion which is inherent in all beings, as it were?

Rinpoche: Sometimes it is distinguished into Relative Bodhicitta, which is then the compassion, and Ultimate Bodhicitta, which is the wisdom. When you talk about a Buddha or a fully-enlightened Being, then there is limitless compassion and limitless wisdom, but each is not different from the other. Compassion helps to generate wisdom and the more compassionate you become, the more your wisdom becomes stronger and clearer. Greater wisdom then makes the compassion stronger; the compassion becomes *real* and free from stains.

So, therefore, in a way, to have complete or perfect compassion, there has to be wisdom. If there is no wisdom, even if we have very good compassion, there is still a sense of '*I* am *the one* who is compassionate to these poor people.' There has to be at least a little bit of pride, some grasping, some looking down on people if you are thinking like this, which means the compassion cannot be completely unconditional or completely non-grasping.

Student: Is there one aspect of compassion, which is in some sense, 'fabricated?' And the other is 'un-fabricated?' Or could you say that wisdom and compassion are not really two?

Rinpoche: I don't know if you can use the word 'fabricated.' Maybe compassion could be 'fabricated' in a sense, if it was not genuine or not really felt. We could use such a word if we were talking about how strong, or genuine or *real*, the compassion is. As long as we have this experience or understanding of not knowing clearly who we are and how our mind is, as long as we have a dualistic sense of understanding, then our compassion cannot be completely and fully without any sense of self-centredness.

So, therefore, the idea is to bring both together; to develop the compassion and the wisdom together. Ultimate compassion is not like, '*I* feel sorry for *these people* who are suffering.' It is a different way of feeling, because you don't have a feeling of 'I,' so the compassion is not looking down on someone or feeling uneasy or anything like that. It is more of a radiance. You could say, a radiance of love.

That is why, sometimes in the tantras, that kind of compassion is termed as 'Great Bliss' and descriptions like that. This kind of compassion is not about an object of suffering. Maybe our everyday compassion is more about focusing on suffering, about something bad that is happening to someone and we don't want them to suffer; we wish we could do something about their suffering. This is how we start to develop compassion, and that is a good thing. But ultimate compassion does not have any 'stain' of such dualistic thinking left, whatsoever.

We first develop compassion from our own experience that we don't want to suffer, I think, so we don't want others to suffer. This is very basic in our being and shows that really everybody loves himself or herself. Often Westerners say to me, 'I don't love myself,' but I don't understand when they say that. I think, 'Why don't you love yourself? If you don't love yourself, then who *do* you love?'

I think, really, everybody loves himself or herself. I wonder if those who say they don't love themselves, actually they love themselves too much! They not only love themselves too much, they expect too much of themselves. It is like they are in a sulk with themselves! Just like how, if your very good friend or someone with whom you are very close, if they don't do as you wish them to, then you might sulk.

I think this is exactly what is happening when people experience that they don't love themselves - they are actually sulking with themselves. Because they don't think they are good enough and they have too high expectations of themselves - 'I should be much better than this!' It is not that they don't love themselves. They just find they are not exactly what they wanted to be or expected to be. So they sulk, 'I am not talking to you!' This is what I have been thinking recently.

Student: Certain teachings on 'View' talk about basic true nature or self-knowing awareness, saying it 'functions as all-permeating compassion.'

Rinpoche: Yes.

Student: So, is it like a universal force, in a way?

Rinpoche: This way of talking about it is something that we come across in any kind of high-level tantra, or visualisation, practices. These start with the view, which is the understanding of emptiness. Then the compassion arises out of that. First, you are reminding yourself of the fact that everything does not exist on its own; everything is appearance and emptiness. Our mind is empty in its nature too, in this way. Then it also has this quality of clarity or luminosity. That clarity manifests as compassion.

Of course, we cannot fully imagine the boundless capacity of a fully-enlightened Being, but we can try to feel what it is like when we feel very relaxed, very fortunate, there are no problems at all, everything is okay; then there is a feeling of...what would you call it? I think we could say 'kindness.' What is the feeling of kindness? Kindness is some kind of a feeling when you feel benevolent towards everybody. You want good for everybody. You feel positive and helpful towards everybody, because you are completely happy and joyful.

This is maybe a very limited example, but something like that; when you have no negative feeling towards anybody and you are completely having the *most* kind, *most* benevolent, *most* wonderful, *most* loving and *most* compassionate feeling towards all and everybody – how would you feel then? When you understand the nature of emptiness, you don't feel like you have to protect yourself or get anything for yourself or get rid of anything; and that feeling is the essence of your true nature or Buddhanature.

That then manifests something. In visualisation practice, that is what manifests the seed syllable or symbol, which then manifests as a Buddha or a Deity or your Guru, or whatever. This is the practice. In every practice, it is the same. We start the practice from that kind of essence, which is compassion.

Kindness and Compassion From an Ultimate Perspective

Seeds of boundless love and compassion

We have been looking at kindness and compassion and how important these qualities are. But kindness and compassion are not always so easy. They are not found easily and they are not something that we can easily express. When we talk about all beings having Buddhanature, sometimes people think it means that everybody should be feeling completely compassionate all the time – because they have Buddhanature. But that is not the idea. It is very obvious it is not like that. Compassion is something rare and something very precious, especially boundless compassion.

Everybody has love; everybody has some kind of love. That love may be mixed up with lots of attachment and other emotions, but it is there. But *pure* compassion, and *acting* with pure compassion, especially towards people that are not close to us, is not common. And, therefore, it is valuable. It is important; it is desirable. It needs to be cultivated. It needs to be increased. It is something that is very good because, if people had more compassion, it would be the solution to most of our human problems, problems that we ourselves have created.

The reason we say every being has Buddhanature is because, no matter how impure or how limited it is, we all have that seed of love and compassion. Maybe we can only express a very corrupted kind of love, which is very limited and very partial, but the seed for pure love and compassion exists in us all. There is nobody who does not have any love. Everybody wants to be loved; everybody needs love. The fact that we are here, that we are able and grown-up, that we are tall and fat and healthy, is because of somebody's love. Human beings live by the love of others. If we didn't have anybody to take care of us, with love, maybe we would not have survived. The fact that we are here, that seven billion people are here, is evidence of love.

So, therefore, that love is there. But our love is very limited, very partial: we make a demarcation, 'These are the people I love and these are the people I don't love.' 'Here is the part I love and here is the part

I don't love.' In Tibetan, actually, there is no word for 'stranger.' There are words that mean a person who is 'not introduced' or 'not recognised,' but not a 'stranger.' The Buddhist attitude is that everyone is the same – someone who you don't know, or don't recognise now, could have been close to you in another life. They could even have been your mother, or your father, or your child. Someone who you are close to could harm you; while someone you are not close to could do something very kind for you. Everyone is seen as equal in this way. There's an equal potential.

The problem with saying, 'These are the people I love and these people I do not love,' is that it becomes very easy for us to hate those we don't love. And then we change these demarcations very easily also: we can hate someone we used to love and we can love someone we used to hate. This shows how artificial our whole idea of these demarcations is. There is no fixed reality that 'these are the only people I love and those I will never love.'

Sometimes people say Buddhists talk about kindness and compassion a lot, but they don't actually have that much kindness or compassion. I think that is not true, however. Buddhists have compassion. It may not be great, but everybody has compassion. Some have more compassion towards animals than human beings, maybe, but everybody has compassion. Some people might have some level of compassion but maybe not enough to actually go out and do things for people. That also happens. Sometimes we may not go and do, or give, lots of things; but in our heart we have a good wish towards everybody, a benevolent and kind feeling. That, too, is compassion.

So, there are different degrees of compassion and different styles of expressing it. People may not have complete or perfect compassion, but I still think it is important to appreciate whatever compassion they do have. I feel that, if there is a little kindness, a little good heart, a little feeling of helpfulness or wishing well to people, that is compassion; that is kindness. And we should really appreciate that. Even if someone simply shows us the way somewhere, earnestly, I think we should appreciate that.

Appreciating whatever compassion we encounter helps us to develop our own compassion. Having very high expectations, and then always criticising and complaining about other people, is not the way. I think sometimes we receive teachings, or we study, about compassion and we agree how important it is. And then we find somebody who is not being compassionate, maybe they are a little bit angry or something, and we think, 'Oh, how can they be so uncompassionate! It is very bad. There is nobody who is compassionate…'

This attitude does not help. It makes things even worse. Then it may even be better not to listen to teachings about compassion. Because, if learning about compassion encourages us to have higher expectations, instead of valuing and appreciating any little act of compassion, it is not helpful. If we expect everybody to be completely compassionate, we will easily get upset, agitated and disturbed when they are not. That does not make our compassion grow. It can even bring anger and encourage seeing the bad in others. Once you are thinking like this, you are on the road to unhappiness and even depression. None of this helps anything. Instead it is important to understand samsara, to understand the sufferings inherent in life.

We all have our own kinds of problems and weaknesses and negativity. This is how we have been behaving all our life, and for many lifetimes before. It is nothing special, it is normal. It doesn't mean I should not change – I should. But there is no need to feel guilty or beat yourself up about it. It is not something new; you have not suddenly become bad. This is something that has been there all the time. I am like this, at this moment. But if I am able to change, even a little bit, and have a little more positive thoughts or emotions, or do anything better than I have been doing, then I should say, 'Ah, that is great! I have done something better!' We should really appreciate that.

Our steps need to be small steps, and we should not expect too much. Then we will not get so frustrated with the world around us. We will not think everybody should be very compassionate and be disappointed when they are not. Everything is comparative: compared to one thing, something may be worse but, compared to another thing, it is better. So there is nothing called 'good' or 'bad.' If my expectation is not overly high, then whatever I find may be good enough. If my expectation is very high, then whatever I find may never be good enough.

Many people expect Buddhist centres to be full of compassionate and kind and nice people. But then they find they are not and are cross, 'How come it is like that? Why isn't everyone kind and compassionate all the time at Buddhist centres?' People have asked me about this and I have thought up an answer to this question. It is not totally correct but it kind of shows something. This is what I say:

'When you go to the hospital, do you expect everybody to be healthy?' People reply, 'No, of course not.' 'It is the same at Buddhist centres,' I say. A Buddhist centre is not a place where all the compassionate people are. A Buddhist centre is where people go *to become* compassionate. It is the same reason why people go to the hospital to become healthy. So, as you cannot find healthy people in a hospital, you cannot find compassionate people in a Buddhist centre!

I am kind of joking. People cannot argue too much with this answer, but actually I think it is not really true. It is not that people in Buddhist centres are less compassionate or less kind. It is just that people have more expectation. The Buddha's teaching is all about compassion: how to become more peaceful and compassionate and kind. So then, people expect everyone in the Dharma to be very, very compassionate; and kind and peaceful and joyful. And then they come and they find it is not exactly like that. They wonder, 'Why are they so uncompassionate?' But it is not that they are particularly uncompassionate. They are just like everybody else, they are just normal. We have to realise this.

Relative Bodhicitta, or compassion, is the most important thing. Because it is something which is understandable for us. We can see very clearly how important compassion is for ourselves, for others and for the world. Helping others is very important but compassion is not only about helping others. It also influences how we ourselves feel. If I have less anger, less hatred, less ill-will, I am a happier person. If I have anger, hatred, ill-will, jealousy, I am an unhappy person. It is as simple as that. I want to be a happier person so, even if I am only thinking about myself, I should try to be a little bit more compassionate, a little bit kinder.

Understanding Ultimate Bodhicitta

Although the practice of kindness and compassion is the most important thing, compared to the theory, our understanding does play an important part in how we react. If we deeply understand, 'This is the best way of reacting,' then sooner or later we will start to react in that way. The deepest understanding is called Ultimate Bodhicitta. I am reluctant to talk too much about Ultimate Bodhicitta, because of the nature of this subject. I can say lots of things, because I have heard lots of things, but I don't know how useful it is to talk about things unless we can really understand them. But, because this deep understanding offers the real solution, if we can understand it, I will say some words here.

The more peaceful your mind is, the more kind your mind is, the less agitation you have, the less anger and hatred and ill-will you have; the less your mind is grasping, running away from things and running after things, the more peaceful and joyful and compassionate and kind, the more truly happy, your mind will be. If we look at compassion in a deep way, we see that compassion is a very open state of mind, a state of open-heartedness. If you want true happiness, the highest level of happiness, you need to wish well for all others. If you only wish well for yourself, this is actually the basis for all your suffering and problems. 'I want this. I want this. I want this.' This does not give me happiness; it brings me agitation. For example, 'I want happiness. I want happiness...' Or even, 'I want to be compassionate. I want to be compassionate... I am not compassionate enough. I want to be more compassionate!'

There is something the Buddha is supposed to have said; I don't think it is exactly correct that he said it, but it is still helpful: Someone asked the Buddha, 'I want happiness. How do I get happiness?' And the reply was, 'First you get rid of 'I' because that's ego. Then you get rid of 'want' because that's attachment. Now you have happiness.' The more we identify with an 'I' - I want happiness, I want to be compassionate, I want to be the one who can help - the more problems arise. As long as there is this strong grasping with lots of 'I' in it, it is not true compassion. There is too much self in it, too much self-centredness.

How can we have complete, perfect compassion, without any kind of a stain? There would need to be no self-centredness, no ego, no attachment, no clinging to anything. How can you get to this state? That is the issue. That is the point. And that is why we talk also about Ultimate Bodhicitta. Ultimate Bodhicitta is egoless, without self-centredness, fully selfless, with no grasping and no clinging. Not too much 'I.' That can only happen when you understand truly the way you are, the way everything is, the way your mind is.

That is why having some experience of the ultimate nature of things, how I really exist, how everything really exists; to have *experiential* understanding of this, brings selflessness. The clearer your understanding, the less self-centredness you have and the less selfishness. And then the compassion becomes purer and purer. There is no need even to feel 'I am compassionate,' there is simply nothing else left to do, other than doing something for other beings, for everybody.

I see very clearly that, when you look into the life of any great master, any great prophet or saint anywhere in the world, whatever their teachings may be, the characteristic they all share is that they have no selfishness, no self-centredness. I think that is the only real, true sign of a saint or prophet, of a realised being. If they are self-centred, then I don't think they are really a holy being. And that is about Ultimate Bodhicitta.

Ultimate Bodhicitta is very much related, in Buddhist terms, to inner understanding, to understanding Right View and the true nature of things. That is why, when we talk about Ultimate Bodhicitta, we talk about emptiness, we talk about interdependence, we talk about the nature of mind, we talk about meditating on these. And this can really bring pure and completely perfect compassion.

Now, how to get there? How to work on that? There are two ways, or two things we engage with: understanding and meditation. Understanding is sometimes through reflection and investigation. We ask, 'What am I? What is the nature of things, especially myself?' And here there are two ways of investigating: the Madhyamika way, or through pith instruction, as in Mahamudra and Dzogchen.

The Mahamudra way is that you first look at everything, at how things are. All the things around me, how do they exist? Not the details, but the *nature* of things. Then we see that everything is changing. Is there anything that does not change? Everything changes. There is nothing that does not change.

Why does everything change? Because nothing exists on its own, nothing exists independently. Everything is interdependent. Everything is made up of many elements, many causes, many conditions, and is also affected by many things. There is nothing that is not affected by other things. So, therefore, all things change.

Things change, and actually things change *so much* that it is very difficult to find anything existing on its own. Take a flower, for example: first there is nothing, then there is a little bit of a green shoot, like grass; it gets bigger, then there are all these colourful things; then it is shrivelled; then there is no flower; then, again, something grows. And so it goes, on and on. It is like a flow. And not only flowers, we are also like that.

We are always changing. Our body, which we think is so completely there, is always changing. When I was born, I was so small; now look at me – ninety kilos! Every cell of the body is changing all the time. They say that, in seven years, every cell of your body is replaced. I must have completely changed every cell of my body nine times over.

So, that goes to show: What is it that I am? What am I? I am not one thing; I am not existing on my own. I am an interdependent reality, always changing. I can say, 'This is me.' But there is nothing I can identify that is really *me*, in my body. If I can't say 'me,' then I can't say 'mine.' What is 'mine?' – just a concept. This is sometimes called emptiness, or interdependence, which is not just a kind of concept; it is how we are.

Then there is my consciousness: that is also always changing. This moment, one thought or emotion; the next moment, another thought, another emotion. It is changing all the time. So, what is it? We assume there is something called 'I.' But that is an assumption. Where is the 'I?' I have an interdependent experience of seeing, hearing. But is there an independent 'seer' somewhere in my experience?

I cannot find one. You cannot find one. Buddha could not find one. Scientists cannot find one. So, where is it? It is an assumption. We often call it 'ego' in Buddhist terminology. Ego is an assumption of something concrete – me – truly existing somewhere in my body. And because of this assumption – 'this is me' – I feel I need to protect it, I feel fear: 'Something might happen… something should not happen… aaah, I am worried…'

All aversion and attachment is based on this slightly confused, wrong way of seeing things. But it is very strong, this way of seeing things; so much so that it is like an addiction. We have been trying to confirm and reconfirm the existence of 'me' since beginningless time: 'I must be there. I should be there. It cannot be that I am not there. I am me. I am me. I am me.' If you don't look at me, I feel, 'Why don't you look at *me*?' If you don't say hello to me, 'Why don't you say hello to *me*?' We are totally addicted to this. And that is the basis of samsara.

It is the basis of all our problems. Because aversion and attachment come from here. Worry comes from here. Fear comes from here. All our sufferings come from here. Because everything is changing, and that is natural, but we don't want that. We want something else: 'I am changing, but I should not be changing. I want to live long, but I don't want to get old. I am not happy at all to be getting old.' Never tell anyone they look old!

Intellectual understanding of all this is relatively easy but practical understanding is what is very difficult. Firstly, because we don't *want* to understand this. We like to have something to hold onto that is me. Although, in a real sense, if you don't have to hold onto anything that is the nicest, because then there is nothing to fear for. But we have this way of thinking, 'If there is nothing... it would be terrible!' Even if we want to let go of this way of seeing, it is very difficult. We have so much habitual tendency to see in this way. We have seen in this way, and reacted in this way, *so much*, it is impossible to react without this view, impossible to think or feel without it. It would be something totally new; not what we are used to. We like to do what we are used to. Even taking the example of food; everyone likes to eat what they are used to, don't they?

We like what we are used to. But food is nothing compared to our own identity. Sometimes people go through a trauma or something like that and they take it and identify with it until it becomes very difficult to let go of or heal. That is the problem with ego – it's very difficult to let go of – but if we can let go of ego, then we are enlightened. It is just that; enlightenment is about that: to really, fully understand what we are and to relate with it directly and experientially. That frees us.

Then there is no need to have a sense of attachment or aversion at all. It doesn't stop us from being conscious and having clarity of consciousness. Actually, it makes our consciousness a hundred times clearer. Because then I am not making things so small: 'me' and 'others.' The capacity of our mind can be fully used. Even now, scientists, and people generally, say that people do not use a fraction of their brain that they could use. That is because we make ourselves so small and hold onto that. It is like an imprisonment. But if we can free ourselves from that, then the capacity, not only of compassion, but also of wisdom and creativity and the energy of our mind, becomes unlimited.

This is very hard for us to understand; not to mention experience. Now we have looked a little at the understanding of Ultimate Bodhicitta. The next step we will look at is how to experience it; how to meditate on it. That comes next.

Approaching Ultimate Bodhicitta

We've looked a little at the View, the investigation, analysis and understanding of Ultimate Bodhicitta. This is very important, because this is what we call the perfection of wisdom. When we talk about the Six Paramitas or the perfection of wisdom or transcendental wisdom, we are talking about this wisdom. It is paramount because, without this, the other Paramitas [namely Generosity, Morality, Patience, Diligence and Meditation] do not become 'Paramita' - perfect or transcendental. Ultimate Bodhicitta is the wisdom aspect.

We commonly say that the root cause of samsara is ignorance, and the only way to free yourself from ignorance is through wisdom. When we say that, we are talking about this wisdom. But then, in another way, every Dharma practice we do, either directly or indirectly, helps this. When we are doing something like a positive deed or lessening our negative emotions, that is also, directly or indirectly, contributing towards wisdom. Because the reason why we have so much ignorance, and why it is so difficult to experience our wisdom, is because of our thick, thick negative karma and habitual tendencies. Karma is basically habit. So, if we can lessen this negativity a little, bring a little bit of positivity and compassion, this helps to develop wisdom.

Compassion is directly linked to wisdom. The more compassion we have, the less self-clinging or self-centredness we have. I have said many times, that the opposite of all negative emotions is compassion. The more compassion there is, the less hatred, the less anger, the less ill will, there is. More compassion, less jealousy. More compassion, less arrogance. More compassion, less greed. More compassion, less attachment. And, in this way, more compassion, less self-centredness and less selfishness. So, therefore, compassion directly contributes towards wisdom. Wisdom is not only a theoretical, conceptual way of seeing. It is about our experiential way of being. So, the question is, 'How can we be without self-centredness and selfishness?'

This is very important to understand because it describes why we do all those positive things, like reducing negative actions and emotions, and increasing positive actions and emotions. Sometimes we call this purification and accumulation. It is all working directly towards arriving at this wisdom. And, at the same time, wisdom helps in all these areas too. So, it is interdependent. Wisdom helps bring more compassion. Compassion helps bring more wisdom. Doing positive things increases our compassion. Compassion helps us do more positive actions and experience more positive emotions. They say that the strongest method of purification is wisdom, because, once true wisdom is completely experienced and realised, then it is all finished, everything is purified. There is no further need to purify. So, therefore, wisdom is the strongest method. But secondly, compassion is the next strongest, because of this link.

I will discuss a little more here about how to meditate on this wisdom, on Ultimate Bodhicitta. In one way, everything we discussed already is also a meditation: we analyse, we investigate, we try to understand, and then whatever we understand or have some kind of an insight into, then we allow our mind to remain in that. That is also a kind of meditation. And there are many analytical meditations which look at each of these steps; letting our mind completely relax and be absorbed in contemplating each step.

Meditating on impermanence is a good example: to meditate on impermanence is regarded as very important. Buddha had a particular way of phrasing things and how he said it was,

'Of all the footprints, the most impressive is that of the elephant. And of all meditations, the most impressive or important one, is that of impermanence.'

I'm not sure I understand his example exactly, but he was saying that meditating on impermanence is extremely important. And there have been great masters that meditated solely on impermanence and, through that, became fully realised.

The challenge is not that we don't understand impermanence. Impermanence is too obvious for us not to understand it. We understand it to some extent, because we know that everything changes and so forth. But that understanding is generally theoretical, in the head. It is not in the heart. We know that everybody dies but we don't really live in the experience that, 'I could die today.' It is too much for us to appreciate fully. We don't *want* to think like that. Much of our ignorance is not just that we don't understand but that we refuse to understand. We don't want to understand or think about impermanence. Everything is so uncertain and so changing. We know that, but we don't want to accept it. We like to think that everything remains as it is and nothing changes. 'I will live for a thousand years and still feel young!' We may not think exactly like this but we do have this kind of feeling.

So, therefore, when people meditate on impermanence, they really try to bring this understanding from their head to their heart. Sometimes people say the longest journey is from your head to your heart, and in many ways it is true. Understanding something from your head and understanding it from your heart are two different things. If we really understood impermanence from our heart, then we would actually learn how to live our life very happily, because we would know that what we have is just these moments, nothing else.

Moments

One of my favourite stories these days is one about moments, which I heard recently. It goes like this: A person died and God, or God's agent, came and said, "Let's go now." But the person did not want to go:

"I have many things to do. I have many plans and projects; I cannot go now!"

"There is no choice," said the agent, "You are dead. You have to go."

So, he had to go with him, unhappily. Then he saw that the agent was carrying a box. So he asked, "What is in that box?"

"Everything that you have is in here."

Then he got interested. "You mean all my things like my money and my belongings, things like that?"

"No, no; they never belonged to you actually. They belonged to the earth. You never had them anyway."

"Oh. Then, is it my friends and relatives, things like that?"

"No, no. They never belonged to you. Maybe they belonged to your heart."

"Then, is it my talents, and my knowledge?"

"They didn't belong to you. They just belonged to the circumstances."

"Then it must be my soul?"

"No, your soul doesn't belong to you. It belongs to God."

"Then what is in there? I want to see! Can I see?"

"Yes, if you want to see, you can just look in. It is open. It is not locked."

So, he opened the box and it was completely empty. There was nothing inside it. Then he asked, "So you mean I don't own anything? Is there nothing that I own?"

"No, you don't own anything. You don't have anything. You never owned anything."

"But what did I have then, after all?"

"You had moments. You just had some moments. And you wasted them and now they are finished."

So that is how it is; our life. We have some moments, and moments go very fast. But these are the only moments we have. Now is the only moment we have. Past is gone. Future is not there. This moment... this moment... this moment. Which means it is not useful to think too much about the past or think too much about the future. It is all about *these moments* and how we use them. How we live in these moments. That makes up what we are.

But, most of the time, we just waste these moments. Sometimes by thinking about the past and becoming miserable about what happened in the past. Sometimes by thinking about the future and getting so worried about what might, or should, or should not, happen in the future. And we never live each moment by each moment, now.

If we really understood impermanence, then we would use these moments. Because we don't have anything else. And in these moments we have, we would be nice, we would be kind, we would enjoy, we would love each other, we would help each other. Because there is nothing else. We don't have anything else. We can't do anything else. The past is gone; there is nothing we can do about it. That is why they say, 'Past is history, future is mystery, present is a gift; therefore, we call it 'present.'

Sometimes people think that if we meditate or reflect on impermanence, then it will make us feel sad and unpleasant, because everything changes. In the beginning it can make us sad, because we have so much illusion and expectation that things should not change. Or that they should remain largely the same and only change a little bit; or only change for the better. But when you really understand impermanence deeply, you become very happy because you realise that there is nothing else other than these present moments. And there is nothing you can do except in these present moments. So it is actually totally useless to think too much about the past or the future. You can make plans; you can have ambitions and make aspirations, no problem. Whatever you wish for might happen; but it might also not happen. If it happens, that's good.

But if it doesn't happen, that is also good. So to think or meditate on impermanence can have a very strong effect.

We have lots of teachings and methods and many different approaches in Buddhism. Some are simple and some are not so simple, but most of the time what really makes a difference is whether we can apply them practically. We often hear teachings and segregate whatever we find easy over to one side and whatever we find difficult or we can't understand, over to the other side, but either way we kind of 'file them away' and forget about them. We don't really practise them; we don't really use them or integrate them with ourselves. Then we never really transform. I might have some understanding but if I don't practise I won't change, I won't transform. So it doesn't actually help.

If I want something to go deep into me and really work on me and transform me, I need to go deeply into it. I need to 'chew on it.' I need to revisit it again and again. I need to really become one with it. I need to learn to experience and react in that way. That is called 'practice.' If I did practise one of the simplest, easiest, most accepted teachings, I think I would benefit more than listening to complicated teachings I cannot practise.

For example, we talk about Precious Human Life: learning to appreciate what we have. This, and this alone, if we really used it on ourselves, would make us much, much happier. Because usually we focus on what we *don't* have. We don't focus on what we do have. We focus on what we *should* have, what we *want* to have, rather than appreciating all the things we *do* have. If we focused our mind on all the good, wonderful things we have, all the opportunities and so on, I think we would become very happy. But we only know this in a theoretical way and we don't use it in our life. *That* is the practice: using these teachings on ourselves and really integrating them with ourselves. Unless we do this, whatever teachings we receive, no matter how high or deep or vast they are; they will not work.

I have received many, many teachings: the deepest, the highest, from many great masters, and I have some intellectual knowledge of them but when it comes down to the real experience, this does not help if you have not meditated enough. One time we were with a special high Lama who was due to give some very special Dzogchen teachings and he kept delaying to give them. People were becoming desperate for them, saying they would do anything if he would give these teachings.

But I was saying to them, 'It is not *so* important; it is not absolutely necessary that you have to receive these teachings. The important thing is to really use whatever teachings you have already received.' Because I have received so many teachings. And the higher the teachings I receive, the more I feel I am going backwards in my own practice, becoming worse. When I receive the highest, the deepest, teachings, I find myself needing to go back to the very beginning of practice. Because I realise that that is what I have to do. If I don't go back and use those most elemental practices, the high teachings do not really work.

So, therefore, all the simple things are extremely important. We can understand them because they are not so difficult to understand. But if we completely integrate them with ourselves, then they can completely transform us. I think that is why great masters don't give these high and deep teachings so easily. It is not because they feel they have this precious thing they do not want to give you, unless you are very nice and very kind. It is not like that. It is because they feel that, unless we practise the simple things, just receiving teachings will not make any difference.

Sometimes it is good to have a little bit of theory, however, because otherwise you are left wondering what might otherwise be said. So, I will say a few words about the meditation on Ultimate Bodhicitta, but bearing all this in mind.

Meditating on Ultimate Bodhicitta

Shamatha or calm abiding meditation is an important part of this practice, as well as the aspect of insight. Because this understanding is all about the mind and, if our mind can't even relax or stay calmly for a few minutes, it is difficult to have any insight into it. But it is not about making our mind completely quiet. It is not about how long you can stay without thinking; or how long you can remain completely quiet. It is not too much about that; it's about our understanding. Because when we look at our mind – 'look' here does not mean looking with our eyes, of course – it is more like when we 'feel' our mind; either the mind is relaxed, stable, resting, quiet, at peace; or it is moving, active, lots of thoughts and emotions, running around.

If the mind is quiet and calm, then who knows that it is calm? Mind itself. Because the mind is basically an awareness, a knowing thing, a clarity. So, when your mind is calm, it knows it is calm. Now, the one who knows it is calm and the one that is calm; is that two things or one thing? There is nothing like 'one mind saying it is calm' and 'another mind which is calm.' The mind itself is calm.

Now, when the mind is not calm, when it is active, moving; who knows that it is moving? It knows itself. That awareness is there. That awareness *is* the mind; it is the basis. Either the mind is calm or it is active. When it is calm, that is the mind. And then the thoughts and emotions and movement, that is also mind. It is the same; just different aspects, different manifestations, differently shown.

An example that is commonly given is that of the ocean: When the ocean is calm and when there are waves in the ocean, it is still just the same ocean. The waves are not separate, or apart from, the ocean. They are the same thing. It is not something coming out from somewhere else. It is just that same water, in a different manifestation. It is the same with our mind. When it is calm, it is like there are no waves. When it is active, it is like waves coming.

So, our mind is there, conscious; sometimes calm, sometimes not calm. But however rough it is, that is not coming from anywhere else. It is just awareness itself. There is nothing else. That awareness is there. If we can just watch and look at that awareness, that awareness that is feeling the calmness or feeling the waviness, the movement or activity; that awareness itself is calm. Whatever thoughts or emotions there are, they are manifesting out of that, coming out of it like bubbles, and dissolving back within it like bubbles. However strong an emotion might be, however strong a thought might be, whatever forcefulness arises, it is not from outside. It all arises from within the mind.

When we deeply understand this, we see that our happiness is just one manifestation of our mind. Our unhappiness is another manifestation. Any thought is just a manifestation: fear, joy, happiness, sadness, anger, greed, selfishness, self-centredness, compassion, kindness – they are all just waves coming out of this awareness. And they all come, and then dissolve, within that. So, actually in one way, it is not necessary that we make our mind calm. Whether it is calm or it is not calm, doesn't make too much difference. Each one is just another aspect.

The only thing is that we should not be afraid of those waves. Usually we think as if, 'Oh, there is a wave, it is very bad...' But when you understand that you yourself are the ocean, then you don't have to be afraid of the waves. It is just like how, once you are in the water, you can no longer 'get wet.' Your mind is the ocean so you don't have to be afraid of the waves – they are yourself. They are just another manifestation of your awareness. When I deeply understand this, selfishness, enlightenment, anything we call it, all my experience is a manifestation of my mind. There is nothing really 'good' or 'bad.' They all arise and they all dissolve within that awareness.

So, therefore, it is not really necessary to run after something or run away from something else. Because we cannot do it anyway. And we don't need to do it. Because, if a thought or feeling arises, it dissolves again. We think, 'Ah, but I have to go and get such and such...' But there is really nowhere to go and nothing to get, and actually nobody to get it. It is the same with running away – there is nothing to run away from and there is nobody to run away. So, all these things could be called illusions, or manifestations. That is why sometimes the great masters say,

> *'All this samsara and nirvana;*
> *All these good things and bad things;*
> *I look at them and I laugh:*
> *I see how creative my mind is.'*

Longchenpa said this. So, when you deeply understand that your mind is nothing but that awareness, then you deeply realise there is nothing to get and nothing to get rid of. That is why it says in the Prajnaparamita Sutra:

> *'There is no good thing;*
> *No bad thing;*
> *Nothing to get;*
> *Nothing to lose;*
> *Nothing to arise;*
> *Nothing not to arise.'*

That understanding is the greatest mantra. It is the highest solution. It is the salvation. It is the freedom. So, in a way, there is also nothing to meditate on. There is nothing to 'meditate' once you understand or realise this. Sometimes it is said:

> *'There is nothing to meditate;*
> *But you have to meditate a lot.'*

But that understanding or clarity has to become part of ourselves, and that is the meditation. Sometimes, when pith instructions are given, like in Mahamudra or Dzogchen, you try to experience this, try to understand this. But the real understanding of this is dependent on many things, as I have said - on purification, on accumulation, on having a good karmic connection. Sometimes it is said that, if a very highly realised great master meets an open and ripe student, saying just one word is enough. Machig Labdrön, the great Tibetan female master who founded the Chöd practice, was an example of this.

Paths to realisation

Machig Labdrön was born to a more-or-less ordinary family. She received some education on how to read and became a very fast reader. In Tibet, there is a tradition of reciting all the texts of the Buddha – one hundred volumes! – and especially the twelve or eighteen volumes of the Prajnaparamita Sutras. People bring monks and nuns to read all these sutras from beginning to end, in the hope it will clear all their obstacles. That is the Tibetan tradition.

So, people in her area used to request Machig Labdrön to come and read because she was very fast. She was much faster than the Lamas in her area so it was relatively inexpensive for the people. I don't even think she was given very much donation in exchange; she was like the girl next door whom everyone asked to just come and read some Prajnaparamita Sutras for them. Maybe they gave her some food in return or something.

She read these sutras so many times, that she learnt them and practically memorised them. And then one day, a great Indian master called Padampa Sangyé came, and he gave one instruction and she became realised. She needed only one instruction because she was so ready, so ripe. She became a yogi and a teacher. And her Chöd practice became the most popular practice in Tibet. It was taken up by all four schools of Tibetan Buddhism and even the Bonpos practised it. She was a most revered Tibetan Lama, and revered by all schools.

Yet sometimes this process takes a very long time, and needs a lot more than just one instruction; it needs years and years of meditation and so forth. It depends on each person. But this is the kind of meditation we have been talking about. And of course, it is not really about the words. There is no certainty as to what actually triggers someone to have the experience. Sometimes the most unexpected happening can make you have the most profound realisation, when the right conditions come together.

You know about the story of Tilopa and Naropa? Naropa was one of the greatest and most learned professors of Nalanda University. He was known to be especially good at tantras, the highest and deepest teachings. Then, one day, he was sitting in the sun, reading a very complicated tantra. And he was saying to himself, 'People say I am a really great scholar, who understands everything and it is true. I understand everything, even the most complicated things.'

At that moment, a shadow fell over his book and he looked up. There was an old woman, haggard-looking, with a long nose, so long that it looked like it had nine bends in it. She was not actually saying anything but her eyes were saying, 'You don't really understand anything.' And when he looked at her, he realised this was true. He realised he understood all the words but he did not have the ultimate, or real, experience. 'I only understand the words,' he thought to himself, and completely understood this to be the case.

"Who then understands?" he asked.

She said, "My brother, Tilopa." And she disappeared.

Naropa stood up and, without even closing his book, he walked away, in search of Tilopa. No resignation to the university. No warning to anyone. No notice. He just disappeared, in search of Tilopa. And, after a long, long search, he found him. But he found him in a not-very-inspiring situation. Tilopa was just at the banks of the Ganges, catching fishes with his bare hands; putting them on the fire even before they were dead. So he was killing fish in a most gruesome way and then eating them. He didn't look like a Buddhist master at all. But somehow, Naropa had this irreversible faith and he followed him. He followed him for many years - with not even one word of teaching.

Tilopa only gave Naropa trouble, and the worst kind of troubles. He would ask things like, 'Who can jump over this cliff?' And so Naropa would jump over the cliff. Sometimes he would even make Naropa go and kidnap brides from their wedding procession! Of course, Naropa got really thrashed, almost to death as a result. And then, in the end, Tilopa got really angry one time and he took out his shoe – they just had a kind of wooden sandal in those days – and he threw it at Naropa. It hit him on the head and he fainted. When he woke up from that faint, he knew everything. He knew exactly what his teacher knew. He received everything.

So, you never know how or when something happens like that for you. Because it's an experiential thing. It's not about words. It's about purification. Instructions may be necessary but you can get so many instructions and they don't do anything. Then sometimes, something triggers something and it just happens like that. It is basically about purification.

When we do Ngöndro practice, the Preliminary Practices, this is also for that: for realising Ultimate Bodhicitta. The main thing in the Ngöndro is also about that: learning to let go, of the positive as well as the negative. Vajrasattva practice is to let go of all the negative things that you hold onto. Mandala Offering is to let go of all the positive things that you hold onto. Guru Yoga is to let go of your 'self-identity,' through devotion and openness; you open your heart completely. That is the preparation.

This is, more or less, the meditation for Ultimate Bodhicitta. The practice is to practise compassion and kindness - Relative Bodhicitta - as the basis and then to try and use Ultimate Bodhicitta as much as possible. Then, together with the Six Paramitas, to help purify and accumulate, that makes up the whole of practice. It is not so much about formal and informal practice. Sometimes people think that, if you go to a monastery or a Buddhist centre or a retreat, and then you meditate, that is the formal practice. And then, if you don't do that, it is informal. It is not really like that.

Practice is using these teachings in your life. You could call it formal, or you could call it informal, but that is the practice. Of course, coming to a centre or a retreat and doing some meditation is important, but how much that becomes a real practice depends on how much you understand. There is no point if practice just becomes another thing to do, like extra work or more things to fit into your life. We already do lots of things. Just doing one more thing is not really practice. What makes it practice, and what makes a difference, is how much you use it to bring forth compassion and wisdom. It is about how much you integrate the teachings, and your understanding, with yourself and your life.

བྱང་ཆུབ་སེམས་མཆོག་རིན་པོ་ཆེ། །
མ་སྐྱེས་པ་རྣམས་སྐྱེས་གྱུར་ཅིག །
སྐྱེས་པ་ཉམས་པ་མེད་པ་དང༌། །
གོང་ནས་གོང་དུ་འཕེལ་བར་ཤོག །

Bodhicitta, most precious aspiration,
May it blossom in every heart.
Never waning, may it flourish and grow
Ever higher and greater.

Dedication

All my babbling,
In the name of Dharma
Has been set down faithfully
By my dear students of pure vision.

I pray that at least a fraction of the wisdom
Of those enlightened teachers
Who tirelessly trained me
Shines through this mass of incoherence.

May the sincere efforts of all those
Who have worked tirelessly
Result in spreading the true meaning of Dharma
To all who are inspired to know.

May this help dispel the darkness of ignorance
In the minds of all living beings
And lead them to complete realisation
Free from all fear.

Ringu Tulku

Glossary and Notes

Editor's Note: Wherever possible the descriptions in the glossaries of the Heart Wisdom books include Ringu Tulku's own words, gathered from a variety of teaching sources. But, as this is not always possible, the glossary is offered as a help to the reader and not a definitive authority.

Arhat (Sanskrit; *dracompa* Tibetan) literally means 'foe destroyer;' one who has overcome the enemies of conflicting emotions and has realised the non-existence of a personal self; this is the goal of the Sravakayana or Foundational vehicle of Buddhism.

Attachment refers to holding on too strongly to something, clinging to it; you get too close to something you perceive as 'nice' until your relating with it takes on a 'sticky' kind of feeling.

Aversion refers to a mind quality of rejecting or pushing something away; wishing it were not there and trying to eliminate it or get away from it.

Bodhicitta (*Bodhicitta* Sanskrit; *chang chub kyi sem* Tibetan) is the heart essence of the Buddha, of enlightenment. The root of the word, *Bodh*, means 'to know, to have the full understanding' and *citta* refers to the heart-mind or 'heart feeling.' In a practical sense, Bodhicitta is compassion: compassion imbued with wisdom.

Bodhisattva (Sanskrit; *changchub sempa* Tibetan) comes from the root *bodh* which means 'to know, to have the full understanding.' The term describes a being that has made a commitment to work for the benefit of others to bring them to a state of lasting peace and happiness and freedom from all suffering. A Bodhisattva does not have to be a Buddhist but can come from any spiritual tradition or none. The key thing is that they have this compassionate wish to free all beings from suffering, informed by the wisdom of knowing this freedom is possible.

Bonpo (Tibetan) is a person who follows the native Tibetan religion of Bon, which was practised in Tibet before Buddhism was brought there.

Buddhadharma *see Dharma.*

Buddhanature / Buddha nature (*Sugatagarba* Sanskrit; *desheg nyingpo* Tibetan) refers to the fundamental, true nature of all beings, free from all obscurations and distortions. Ultimately, our true nature, and the true nature of all beings, is inseparable from the nature of Buddha. It is the 'primordial goodness' of sentient beings, an innate all-pervasive primordial purity.

Chöd (Tibetan), literally meaning 'cutting through,' is a practice based on the Prajnaparamita Sutra (see below). The realised Tibetan female teacher, Machig Labdrön, set down the system of practice, after having received teachings from the Indian Mahasiddha Padampa Sangyé. The purpose of the practice is to cut through all aversion and attachment, all ego-clinging or clinging to a 'self.'

Deity / Deities (*istadevata* Sanskrit; *yidam* Tibetan) in Buddhism, are representations of the embodiment of enlightened mind. They are visualised or depicted in various forms to bring out different aspects of its essential purity. During formal practice a deity may be visualised in front of or above the practitioner or as the practitioner him or herself. Deities encourage us to see the pure state of reality, by which we mean the state that does not bind us or create problems and is, therefore, a liberating state.

Dharma (Sanskrit; *chö* Tibetan) The word *Dharma* has many uses. In its widest sense, it means all that can be known, or the way things are. The other main meaning is the teachings of the Buddha; also called the *Buddhadharma*. This refers to the entire body of oral and written Buddhist teachings, and includes the literal teachings and that which is learnt through practising them.

Dzogchen (Tibetan; *Ati Yoga* Sanskrit) literally translates as 'Great Completion' or 'Great Perfection.' It is a body of teachings and practices that are considered to be the highest of the Inner Tantra of the Nyingma School of Tibetan Buddhism. They are aimed at helping a practitioner to achieve primordial true nature, the natural state. The practice of Dzogchen ultimately brings the same result as Mahamudra.

Emptiness (*shunyata* Sanskrit; *tong pa nyi* Tibetan) The Buddha taught in the second turning of the wheel of Dharma, that all phenomena have no real, independent existence of their own. They only appear to exist as separate, nameable entities because of the way we commonly, conceptually, see things. But in themselves, all things are 'empty' of inherent existence. This includes our 'self', which we habitually unconsciously mistake to be an independently-existing, separate phenomenon. Instead, everything exists in an interdependent way and this is what the term emptiness refers to. As Ringu Tulku says in *Like Dreams and Clouds*: 'Emptiness does not mean there is nothing; emptiness means the way everything is, the way everything magically manifests.' [Bodhicharya Publications: 2011].

Guru Yoga (*lamay naljor* Tibetan) is the practice of devotion to the guru and, through receiving blessing, visualising blending indivisibly with the mind of the guru.

Habitual tendencies (*She jay drib pa* Tibetan) Literally translated from Tibetan as 'obscurations of knowledge,' these refer to our propensity to act or react in certain ways, reinforced and influenced by past actions. They become ingrained in us again and again until they are habitual.

Kagyu (Tibetan) *Ka* means 'oral' and *gyu* means 'lineage:' the Lineage of Oral Transmission; also known as the 'Lineage of Meaning and Blessing' or the 'Practice Lineage.' It traces its origins to the primordial Buddha, Dorje Chang (Vajradhara) and the great Indian master and yogi, Tilopa. It is one of the four major schools of Tibetan Buddhism, and is headed by H.H. the Karmapa, currently H.H. XVII Karmapa Ogyen Trinley Dorje. The other three main schools are the Gelug, Nyingma, and Sakya.

Karma (Sanskrit; *lay* Tibetan) literally means 'action.' It refers to the cycle of cause and effect that is set up through our actions. Actions coloured or motivated by *klesha*, for example, anger or desire, will tend to create results in keeping with that action and also increase our tendency to do similar actions. These tendencies become ingrained in us and become our habitual way of being, which is our karma. According to our level of awareness, we can change our karma through consciously refining our actions.

Lama (Tibetan; *guru* Sanskrit) means teacher or master. *La* refers to there being nobody higher in terms of spiritual accomplishment and *ma* refers to compassion like a mother. Thus both wisdom and compassion are brought to fruition together in the lama. The word has the connotation of 'heavy' or 'weighty,' indicating the guru or lama is heavy with positive attributes and kindness.

Longchenpa (1308-1364) was one of the most brilliant teachers of the Nyingma lineage and a foremost master of Dzogchen. He is acknowledged by all schools of Tibetan Buddhism as one of Tibet's greatest teachers. His writings cover all aspects of the Buddhist path but his major work is the *Seven Treasures,* which summarises the previous 600 years of Buddhist thought in Tibet. He transmitted the *Longchen Nyingtig* cycle of teachings to Jigme Lingpa, which has become one of the most widely practised. He was abbot of Samye, the first Buddhist monastery in Tibet, but spent most of his life travelling or in retreat. For further information see his biography *Buddha Mind* by Tulku Thondup [Snow Lion: 1989].

Madhyamika (Sanskrit) literally means 'The Middle Way' and is the most influential of four major philosophical schools of Indian Buddhism. This Middle Way avoids falling into the extremes of either eternalism or nihilism.

Mahamudra (Sanskrit; *cha ja chen po* or *chak chen* Tibetan) literally means 'Great Seal' or 'Great Symbol,' referring to the way in which all phenomena are 'sealed' by their primordially perfect true nature. The term can denote the teaching, meditation practice or accomplishment of Mahamudra. The meditation consists in perceiving the mind directly rather than through rational analysis, and relies on a direct introduction to the nature of the essence of the mind. This form of meditation is traced back to Saraha (10th century), and was passed down in the Kagyu school through Marpa. The accomplishment lies in experiencing the non-duality of the phenomenal world and emptiness: perceiving how the two are not separate. This experience can also be called the union of emptiness and luminosity.

Mahayana (Sanskrit; *tek pa chen po* Tibetan) translates as 'Great Vehicle.' This is the second vehicle of Buddhism, and emphasises the teachings on Bodhicitta, compassion, and interdependence. It expands on the teachings of the Sravakayana (the foundational vehicle of Buddhism) and sees the purpose of enlightenment as being the liberation of *all* sentient beings from suffering, as well as oneself. This is the path of the Bodhisattva (see above) and so may also be called the Bodhisattvayana.

Mandala Offering (Sanskrit; *kyil khor* Tibetan) is an offering that is visualised as the entire universe. It traditionally comprises thirty-seven aspects and is often made as part of a request to receive Dharma teachings; one of the Four Extraordinary Foundational practices of the Ngöndro. See *Ngöndro*.

Mantra (Sanskrit; *ngag* Tibetan) The word mantra is an abbreviation of two syllables *mana* and *tara*, respectively meaning 'mind' and 'protection:' coming from the mind, giving protection through transformation. Mantras are Sanskrit words or syllables that express the quintessence of particular energies or of a deity. They protect the mind from distraction and serve as support for meditation.

Marpa (1012-1097 C.E.), known as Marpa the Translator, was born in Tibet and was a householder, married with six sons. He made three trips to India to seek teachings from Naropa, his teacher, and brought back many tantric texts, which he translated from Sanskrit into Tibetan. These include the *Six Yogas of Naropa*, the *Guhyasamaja* and the *Chakrasamvara* practices. He thus founded the Kagyu lineage in Tibet. His main student was Milarepa.

Naropa was a great Indian scholar who lived in the 11th century. He was one of the greatest and most learned professors of Nalanda University and became the main disciple of Tilopa, and guru to Marpa. These are the forefathers of the Kagyu lineage.

Ngöndro (Tibetan) is a series of practices comprising Four Ordinary Foundations and Four Extraordinary Foundations. They were originally created for the Tibetan people by the Indian Mahasiddha, Atisha Dipamkara, and are treated as the gateway to all deep Vajrayana practices. The Ordinary Foundations are contemplations on: precious human birth, death and impermanence, karma, and samsara. The Four Extraordinary Foundations are the recitation of: 100,000 refuge prayers and prostrations, 100,000 Vajrasattva mantras, 100,000 mandala offerings, and 100,000 guru yoga practices. The Ngöndro is practised by all schools of Tibetan Buddhism with slight variations. See *The Ngöndro: Foundation Practices of Mahamudra* by Ringu Tulku [Bodhicharya Publications: 2013].

Nirvana (Sanskrit; *nyangde* Tibetan) literally means 'extinguished' and is the state of being free from all suffering. It is the opposite of samsara and arises when we have completely done away with all the obscurations, misunderstandings, negative emotions and other hindrances that create samsaric existence. When we are free from all fear and suffering and our mind is completely clear; this is described as enlightenment or nirvana.

Paramita / Six Paramitas (Sanskrit; *Parami* Pali) are literally the *'perfections'* which together lay out the path of practice for a Bodhisattva. Generosity is paramount and comes first, the others unfolding one by one from the other, to give the six: Generosity, Morality (Good Conduct or Discipline), Patience, Diligence, Meditation and Wisdom. Wisdom is both the fruition of the other Paramitas and informs the practice of them all.

Prajnaparamita Sutra (Sanskrit) is the teachings on the sixth Paramita or 'perfection,' wisdom (*prajna* Sanskrit). It describes the wisdom of directly realising emptiness, the non-conceptual simplicity of all phenomena. There are several versions of different lengths and many translations into English from different languages.

Rinpoche (Tibetan) is an honorific term in the Tibetan Buddhist tradition, reserved for great masters. It refers to how precious it is that such teachers are among us; literally translating as 'precious one.'

Samsara / samsaric (Sanskrit; *khor wa* Tibetan) is the state of suffering of 'cyclical existence.' It describes a state of mind that experiences gross and / or subtle pain and dissatisfaction. It arises because the mind is deluded and unclear and thus perpetually conditioned by attachment, aversion and ignorance.

Shamatha (Sanskrit; *shiné / shinay* Tibetan) is calm abiding meditation: calming and stabilising the mind to bring it to a state of peace. Sometimes also called tranquillity meditation.

Shantideva (675- 725 C.E.) was a great, and controversial, scholar at the famous Nalanda University in Northern India. He was the author of the *Bodhicharyavatara*, a key Mahayana text, which describes the path of the Bodhisattva.

Sutra/sutras (Sanskrit; *do* Tibetan) are the teachings given by Shakyamuni Buddha, memorised by his disciples and subsequently written down.

Tantra (Sanskrit; *gyü* Tibetan) literally means 'continuity' or continuous thread (of the pure nature of mind) that runs through everything. In Buddhism, it also refers to the meditative practices of the Vajrayana, which include mantra recitation, visualisation practices, and the texts that describe these.

Tilopa was an Indian Mahasiddha, who lived in the 10th and 11th centuries. He was from the area near Dharamsala but travelled around a lot, practising in an inconspicuous way and appearing quite ordinary. He had four main teachers and one meaning of the Kagyu lineage of Tibet, of which he is a founding father, is the

'Four Oral Traditions,' referring to his teachers. He worked pressing sesame seed oil and became enlightened while working in this way. He was the guru of Naropa and passed the Kagyu teachings on to him.

Tonglen (Tibetan) literally means 'sending and taking' and refers to the meditation associated with the Lojong (Mind Training) teachings of the Mahayana Vehicle of Buddhism. One visualises sending out love and happiness and healing light, while taking in the sufferings of the world, visualised as a thick black smoke. The visualisation rides the out and in breath in this way and works on our own mind and our view - our clinging to a self, separate from others, which must be protected over others. The reverse psychology of the meditation thus helps uproot our wrong assumptions, in a tangible and heart-felt way.

Vajrasattva (Sanskrit; *Dorje Sempa* Tibetan) is the Buddha particularly associated with purification, cleansing and letting go of all negativity. He holds a bell and *dorje* (Tibetan; *vajra* Sanskrit) in his left and right hands, which symbolise emptiness and the indestructibility of the true nature of things. See Ringu Tulku's book *Being Pure: The practice of Vajrasattva* [Bodhicharya Publications: 2016].

Notes

1. From: *The Dhammapada: The sayings of the Buddha,* translated by Thomas Byrom. Rider Books: 2008.

Editor's Note: Throughout the Heart Wisdom series we have used the word *student* to identify questions and discussion from audience members. This is not intended to imply the speaker would necessarily identify themselves as a student of Tibetan Buddhism or of Ringu Tulku. It refers to the fact that they are being a 'student,' just in this instance, by virtue of asking a question in order to understand more.

Acknowledgements

Many thanks to Mariette van Lieshout, Maeve O'Sullivan and Anna Howard for proof reading and offering editorial comments which helped greatly in the production of this book. Also thanks, as always, to Rachel Moffitt who oversees printing and distribution of our books and all things administrative in Bodhicharya Publications. And to Paul O'Connor who brings Rinpoche's teachings alive with his beautiful layout and design.

Very many thanks go to Donal Creedon for holding the retreat space in which this book was worked extensively on, and where several pertinent questions are included from. Thank you to all the organisers of the teachings that provided the basis of this book, and the students that asked such insightful questions at them: the retreat at Bodhicharya Meditation Centre, Sikkim, India; Dzogchen Beara, Ireland; Palpung Changchub Dargyeling, Wales and White Tara Group for organising the teaching in Oxford, UK. And thank you to Maitreya House and The Orchard Dharma Centre, Herefordshire, who have accommodated me at various times, while I have pored over this text.

Thank you forever to my family, my husband and daughters, who have taught me about *being* kind. And thank you to Ringu Tulku, without whose deep and limitless kindness these clear teachings would not be available to help us all. Since they have the potency to transform our every momentary experience of life, what greater gift could there be? Thank you Rinpoche.

Mary Dechen Jinpa
On behalf of Bodhicharya Publications
September 2017

About the Author

Ringu Tulku Rinpoche is a Tibetan Buddhist Master of the Kagyu Order. He was trained in all schools of Tibetan Buddhism under many great masters including HH the 16th Gyalwang Karmapa and HH Dilgo Khyentse Rinpoche. He took his formal education at Namgyal Institute of Tibetology, Sikkim and Sampurnananda Sanskrit University, Varanasi, India. He served as Tibetan Textbook Writer and Professor of Tibetan Studies in Sikkim for 25 years.

Since 1990, he has been travelling and teaching Buddhism and meditation in Europe, America, Canada, Australia and Asia. He participates in various interfaith and 'Science and Buddhism' dialogues and many books have now been published of his teachings. These include the *Heart Wisdom* series and the *Lazy Lama* series as well as *Path to Buddhahood, Daring Steps, The Ri-me Philosophy of Jamgon Kongtrul the Great, Confusion Arises as Wisdom, Mind Training, Parables from the Heart* and several children's books, available in Tibetan and European languages.

He founded the organisations Bodhicharya - see www.bodhicharya.org and Rigul Trust - see www.rigultrust.org.

Other books by Ringu Tulku

Published by Bodhicharya Publications:

The Heart Wisdom Series:

- **The Ngöndro**
  Foundation Practices of Mahamudra
- **From Milk to Yoghurt**
  A Recipe for Living and Dying
- **Like Dreams and Clouds**
  *Emptiness and Interdependence;
  Mahamudra and Dzogchen*
- **Dealing with Emotions**
  Scattering the Clouds
- **Journey from Head to Heart**
  Along a Buddhist Path
- **Riding Stormy Waves**
  Victory over the Maras
- **Being Pure**
  The Practice of Vajrasattva
- **Radiance of the Heart**
  Kindness, Compassion, Bodhicitta

The Lazy Lama Series:

- **Buddhist Meditation**
- **The Four Noble Truths**
- **Refuge**
  Finding a Purpose and a Path
- **Bodhichitta**
  Awakening Compassion and Wisdom
- **Living without Fear and Anger**
- **Relaxing in Natural Awareness**
- **Loving Kindness**
  Our true brave heart

Other Titles:

- **Parables from the Heart**
  Teachings in the Tibetan Oral Tradition

Published by Shambhala:

- **Path to Buddhahood**
  Teachings on Gampopa's 'Jewel Ornament of Liberation'
- **Daring Steps**
  Traversing the Path of the Buddha
- **Mind Training**
- **The Ri-Me Philosophy of Jamgon Kongtrul the Great**
  A Study of the Buddhist Lineages of Tibet.
- **Confusion Arises as Wisdom**
  Gampopa's Heart Advice on the Path of Mahamudra.

Also available from Rigul Trust:

- **Chenrezig**
  The Practice of Compassion - A Commentary
- **The Boy who had a Dream**
  An illustrated book for children

For an up to date list of books by Ringu Tulku, please see the Books section at
www.bodhicharya.org

Our professional skills are given free of charge in order to produce these books, and Bodhicharya Publications is run by volunteers; so your purchase of this book goes entirely to fund further books and contribute to humanitarian and educational projects supported by Bodhicharya.

The Ringu Tulku Archive
THE RECORDED TEACHINGS OF RINGU TULKU RINPOCHE

www.bodhicharya.org/teachings